OCCASIONAL PAPER 201

Developments and Challenges in the Caribbean Region

WITHDRAWN

Samuel Itam, Simon Cueva, Erik Lundback,
Janet Stotsky, and Stephen Tokarick

INTERNATIONAL MONETARY FUND
Washington DC
2000

Production: IMF Graphics Section
Figures: Theodore F. Peters, Jr.
Typesetting: Alicia Etchebarne-Bourdin

Cataloging-in-Publication Data

Developments and challenges in the Caribbean region/by Samuel Itam. . . [et
al.].—Washington, D.C.: International Monetary Fund, 2000.

  p. cm.—(Occasional paper, 0251-6365; no. 201).

  ISBN 1-55775-950-2

  1. Caribbean Area—Economic conditions. 2. Monetary policy—
Caribbean Area. 3. Fiscal policy—Caribbean Area. 4. Foreign exchange—
Caribbean Area. 5. Caribbean Area—Commerce. I. Itam, Samuel. II. Inter-
national Monetary Fund. III. Occasional paper (International Monetary
Fund); no. 201.

  HC151 .D493 2000

Price: US$20.00
(US$17.50 to full-time faculty members and
students at universities and colleges)

Please send orders to:
International Monetary Fund, Publication Services
700 19th Street, N.W., Washington, D.C. 20431, U.S.A.
Tel.: (202) 623-7430   Telefax: (202) 623-7201
E-mail: publications@imf.org
Internet: http://www.imf.org

recycled paper

Contents

Tables

Section

Statistical Appendix

The following symbols have been used throughout this paper:

. . .   to indicate that data are not available;

—   to indicate that the figure is zero or less than half the final digit shown, or that the item does not exist;

–   between years or months (e.g., 1998–99 or January–June) to indicate the years or months covered, including the beginning and ending years or months;

/   between years (e.g., 1998/99) to indicate a fiscal (financial) year.

"Billion" means a thousand million.

Minor discrepancies between constituent figures and totals are due to rounding.

The term "country," as used in this paper, does not in all cases refer to a territorial entity that is a state as understood by international law and practice; the term also covers some territorial entities that are not states, but for which statistical data are maintained and provided internationally on a separate and independent basis.

Preface

This occasional paper originated as part of a strategy to enhance policy dialogue between the Caribbean countries and the IMF. It was intended to provide background information for the Article IV consultation discussions of the independent states that are full members of the Caribbean Community (CARICOM), namely, Antigua and Barbuda, The Bahamas, Barbados, Belize, Dominica, Grenada, Guyana, Jamaica, St. Kitts and Nevis, St. Lucia, St. Vincent and the Grenadines, Suriname, and Trinidad and Tobago.

The authors would like to thank colleagues in the Western Hemisphere Department of the IMF for helpful comments on previous drafts and to express gratitude to David Goldsbrough, Ewart Williams, and Frits van Beek for their encouragement and support. They are also grateful for the editing by Esha Ray of the External Relations Department; the processing of the original text, tables, and other materials by Joan Hewitt, Hildi Wicker, and Joan McLeod-Tillman; and the research assistance by Thomas Duffy, Jorge Shepherd, and Ricardo Davico. The views expressed are the sole responsibility of the authors and do not necessarily reflect those of the IMF staff, Executive Directors, or the authorities of the CARICOM countries.

List of Abbreviations

ACP	African, Caribbean, and Pacific countries
CARIFTA	Caribbean Free Trade Association
CARICOM	Caribbean Community
CBI	Caribbean Basin Initiative
CET	Common External Tariff
CSME	Caribbean Single Market and Economy
BIS	Bank for International Settlements
ECCB	Eastern Caribbean Central Bank
EU	European Union
FSF	Financial Stability Forum
GDP	gross domestic product
HIPC	Heavily Indebted Poor Countries
NAFTA	North American Free Trade Agreement
OECD	Organization for Economic Cooperation and Development
OECS	Organization of Eastern Caribbean States
VAT	value-added tax
WTO	World Trade Organization

I Overview

With few exceptions, countries in the Caribbean region have performed reasonably well in recent years. They will, however, need to accelerate policy actions in a number of areas to address the challenges they are likely to face in the near future.

This occasional paper focuses on the independent states that are full members of the Caribbean Community (CARICOM), namely Antigua and Barbuda, The Bahamas, Barbados, Belize, Dominica, Grenada, Guyana, Jamaica, St. Kitts and Nevis, St. Lucia, St. Vincent and the Grenadines, Suriname, and Trinidad and Tobago.[1] It provides background information on recent developments in the Caribbean region and lays out the principal policy issues that countries will need to address in the period ahead. The Caribbean countries[2] face a number of common problems and must deal with similar economic policy issues. Consequently, concentrating on the regional perspective permits a comparison of the individual responses to similar problems. The regional view would also throw light on the countries' movement toward convergence.

Background

Countries in the Caribbean region are small in size, but heterogeneous in structure. Their growth performance was mixed in the 1990s: Belize, Trinidad and Tobago, and member countries of the Organization of Eastern Caribbean States (OECS)[3] enjoyed relatively strong growth, but performance in the others has been uneven. Jamaica has experienced negative growth since 1995.

Caribbean countries have made some progress in diversifying their economies, but production and exports are still relatively concentrated in a few activities. Agriculture and mining remain important in many countries, but the structure of production has begun to shift more heavily toward services. While the number of tourists to the Caribbean has grown in the latter part of the 1990s, growth in tourist receipts has not kept pace with nominal GDP. Growth in the sector has been adversely affected, in part, by natural disasters in the last few years. The market share of the English-speaking countries within the broader Caribbean region has been falling in the 1990s.

Countries in the region are highly open. The principal destinations for the region's exports include the United States, Europe, and other CARICOM countries. Exports are concentrated in a few products, namely raw materials—particularly minerals—and agricultural crops. Imports consist mainly of manufactures, especially consumer goods.

The region's agricultural exports are characterized by high production costs and are sold in protected markets. Caribbean countries have traditionally relied heavily on a system of preferential access to markets for commodities such as bananas and sugar. Most of the countries have large and persistent trade and current account deficits, despite significant current transfers and remittances in some cases, but these deficits have been financed by private capital inflows (including foreign direct investment and commercial borrowing) and, to some extent, official grants.

The commitment to a fixed exchange rate by many of the small island economies in the region has been a key factor in creating a stable macroeconomic framework and in keeping inflation close to international levels. In recent years, all countries (except Suriname) have successfully reduced inflation to single-digit rates. There has been a general trend toward appreciation in the value of the U.S. dollar vis-à-vis other major currencies.

---

[1]The Bahamas is a member of CARICOM but not the Common Market. Haiti is in the formal process of becoming a full member of CARICOM. CARICOM also includes four U.K. territories: Montserrat and Anguilla are members, and the British Virgin Islands and the Turks and Caicos Islands are associate members. Negotiations for a free trade agreement are ongoing between CARICOM and the Dominican Republic, which is, among other Western Hemisphere countries and territories, a CARICOM observer.

[2]In this paper, "Caribbean countries" refer to the group of independent states that are full members of CARICOM.

[3]OECS membership includes six independent countries—Antigua and Barbuda, Dominica, Grenada, St. Kitts and Nevis, St. Lucia, and St. Vincent and the Grenadines—and two U.K. territories—Anguilla and Montserrat.

The banking sector in the region is relatively well developed, compared with other developing countries, but real interest rates remain high because of high reserve and liquidity requirements, generally conservative monetary policies, and—in some cases—large fiscal imbalances. The cost of banking services is relatively high because of the lack of economies of scale, relatively undiversified loan portfolios, and the oligopolistic nature of banking in the region.

In the 1990s, fiscal deficits in the region tended to widen. The average central government deficit rose to 4½ percent of GDP in 1998 from 2 percent of GDP in 1994, mainly as a result of increases in expenditure. Increases in public sector wage bills contributed importantly to the overall increases in expenditure.

Caribbean countries have embarked on a process of economic integration toward the formation of a common market. The area where perhaps the most progress has been made is in trade liberalization. Progress toward fiscal harmonization, adoption of a common currency, and creation of a monetary union have been slower. Since most Caribbean countries trade with countries outside the region, the gains from forming a common market are likely to be small until intraregional trade expands. Furthermore, complex issues regarding convergence to common targets (e.g., on the size of fiscal deficits and the debt-to-GDP ratio) are likely to arise, given the differences that exist across countries in the region.

Challenges Facing the Region

Despite the successes in the 1980s and 1990s in reforming their economies and broadly satisfactory economic performance, Caribbean countries remain vulnerable in a number of ways. Because of their relative openness and concentration on a small range of products, exogenous changes in the terms of trade can have significant effects on their fiscal and external positions. Also, many countries that rely on preferential trading arrangements for their exports are likely to be facing a progressive erosion of these preferences. In addition, occasional natural disasters, such as hurricanes, have the potential to cause serious setbacks for these countries.

In light of their vulnerabilities and the risks to the economic outlook, Caribbean countries will need to take stronger measures to preserve the economic gains made in the past two decades and to provide some measure of insurance against future external shocks. They will need to accelerate policy actions in a number of areas to address the challenges they

are likely to face in the period ahead. Specifically, these countries would need to:

- Deepen financial markets and improve banking sector efficiency, thus reducing the costs of financial intermediation in the region. For this purpose, governments should accelerate privatization of state-owned financial institutions, reduce barriers to entry for new banks that meet prudential standards, and strengthen banking supervision, and privatization of public enterprises.

- Expand trade liberalization to increase the net benefits for the region by further reducing the cost of imports and improving the allocation of resources. Countries will also need to address the likely loss of revenue from liberalization through reforms to their tax systems that broaden and deepen domestic consumption taxation, including introducing a VAT where feasible.

- Improve external competitiveness so as to accelerate growth and reduce unemployment. This can be achieved by restraining production costs, particularly by keeping wage increases in line with growth in productivity.

- Dampen the impact of external shocks by diversifying the structure of exports. Diversification can be encouraged by removing mechanisms that impede markets from working efficiently, such as wage and price controls and restrictive labor laws. Governments should refrain from using subsidies or other incentives that encourage activities for which the country does not have a comparative advantage.

Economic Outlook for the Region

Economic prospects for the region are generally favorable, as growth will likely accelerate somewhat and inflation will remain low over the medium term. Faster growth is likely to come from a number of factors, including higher investment in the energy and tourism sectors and stronger agricultural performance.

The inflation differential with the United States is expected to narrow, resulting in some gains in competitiveness for the region. The combined external current account deficit is likely to improve over the medium term, based on fairly robust growth in the region's export markets and higher prices for the region's major exports. Fiscal balances also are expected to improve, based on strong economic growth and the containment of public sector employment.

This outlook, however, is subject to a number of risks, including slower growth in major export markets, the effects of unpredictable natural disasters, and possible adverse terms of trade shocks.

Section II of this occasional paper discusses the structure of the Caribbean economies in broad terms. Section III presents selected issues facing these countries in greater depth and provides some cross-country analysis. Section IV outlines the economic outlook for the region, focusing on broad economic aggregates and potential risks. Section V contains the main conclusions.

II Economic Background

The economic performance of most of the countries in the Caribbean region has been broadly satisfactory in recent years, but insufficiently robust to substantially reduce unemployment. In the five-year period ended 1998, real GDP growth in the region was somewhat higher than in the major trading partner countries, inflation declined, and the fiscal and external positions improved. Also, progress was made toward trade liberalization.

Growth and Sectoral Structure of Output

The Caribbean countries are relatively small in size and quite heterogeneous in structure. Their combined population is about 6.5 million,[4] with an aggregate GDP of about US$25 billion in 1999. These figures represent approximately 1.3 percent of the total population of the Latin American and Caribbean region and close to 1.2 percent of this broader region's GDP. Average per capita GDP in the Caribbean region was roughly US$3,650 in 1998, ranging from about US$930 in Guyana to approximately US$14,500 in The Bahamas. Table 1 provides some summary economic indicators for the region.[5]

The region's output and population are concentrated in a relatively small number of countries. About 61 percent of the region's population is concentrated in the two largest economies, Jamaica and Trinidad and Tobago, which together account for 54 percent of regional GDP. Two other countries—The Bahamas and Barbados—account for 8½ percent of the population and 27 percent of re-

gional GDP. The six independent member countries of the OECS account for about 8½ percent of the total population of the region and 10 percent of the regional GDP. Finally, continental countries (Belize, Guyana, and Suriname) account for 22 percent of the population, but only 8½ percent of regional GDP.

Since the 1980s, economic performance has varied widely across the region and has been volatile in some countries (Table 2), with Belize, Trinidad and Tobago, and many of the smaller countries (particularly the OECS members) enjoying strong growth, and many of the other economies showing a mixed performance. Despite a recent slowdown for the region as a whole, two of the lower-income countries in the region (Guyana and Suriname) performed well in the mid-1990s, after a steady decline in the 1980s. However, Jamaica—which accounts for about 29 percent of the region's GDP—has experienced a sustained decline in output since the mid-1990s. All countries in the region, except St. Lucia, have experienced at least one year of declining output in the last two decades. The volatility in growth reflects the high degree of vulnerability of these small and relatively undiversified economies to adverse shocks, including frequent natural disasters (Box 1). Unemployment is a problem across many countries in the region, but reliable data are unavailable.

Countries in the Caribbean region have made some progress in diversifying their economies, but production is still relatively concentrated in a few activities. Jamaica's economy is relatively diversified, with agriculture and bauxite together accounting for less than 13 percent of GDP. Likewise, while the petroleum sector is still very important in Trinidad and Tobago, its share in GDP declined during the 1990s and now stands at about 20 percent. The small economies of the region, particularly the OECS countries, rely on agriculture, light manufacturing, tourism, trade, and transportation. Agriculture is also a key sector for the continental economies, together with tourism in Belize and mining in Guyana and Suriname (Table A1).

---

[4]This excludes the most populous countries that lie within the Caribbean Sea that are Spanish- or French-speaking territories, specifically Cuba (11.1 million), the Dominican Republic (8.3 million), and Haiti (7.6 million).

[5]The statistical information provided in this paper is based on data available to the IMF. The coverage and quality of economic statistics, however, could be improved in many of the countries in the region.

Table 1. Caribbean Countries: Summary Indicators
(1994–98 averages, unless otherwise indicated)

	Nominal GDP Per Capita (In thousands of U.S. dollars) 1998[1]	Nominal GDP (In millions of U.S. dollars) 1998	Population (In millions) 1998[2]	Real GDP Growth Rate	Consumer Price Index End of Period (Percent change)	External Current Account Balance (In percent of GDP)	Exports and Imports of Goods and Non-factor Services (In percent of GDP)	Consolidated Public Sector Deficit (In percent of GDP)	Central Government Expenditure (In percent of GDP)
Antigua and Barbuda	8,833	617	0.07	3.5	1.9	–11.2	171.0	–5.4	25.7
The Bahamas	14,450	4,190	0.29	2.4	1.4	–10.3	102.2	–1.4	20.4
Barbados	8,212	2,389	0.27	4.0	2.2	3.5	121.8	0.6	31.7
Belize	2,820	682	0.23	2.4	2.3	–3.3	105.7	–4.3	27.7
Dominica	3,100	260	0.07	2.6	1.4	–12.3	115.6	–1.4	36.3
Grenada	3,209	336	0.10	4.5	1.9	–9.5	111.3	–2.4	31.3
Guyana	932	726	0.77	5.8	8.6	–14.7	211.3	–1.8	39.2
Jamaica	2,604	6,880	2.64	–0.5	23.5	–2.4	122.5	–4.2	32.5
St. Kitts and Nevis	6,935	291	0.04	5.2	4.1	–22.0	147.4	–3.8	34.5
St. Lucia	4,013	610	0.15	2.7	2.8	–8.9	118.2	1.4	27.4
St. Vincent and the Grenadines	2,745	316	0.12	3.2	2.4	–15.3	118.2	–0.3	31.2
Suriname	1,495	640	0.43	7.2	246.4	6.4	174.7	–3.1	40.9
Trinidad and Tobago	4,565	6,083	1.33	4.1	5.0	–2.0	95.8	0.4	27.0
Region[3]	3,684	24,020	6.52	2.6	16.9	–4.3	116.9	–1.7	28.9

Sources: IMF, Recent Economic Developments reports; and IMF staff estimates.

[1] 1997 for Barbados, Belize, and Guyana.

[2] 1997 for Barbados and Belize.

[3] Except for the first three columns, averages weighted by nominal GDP in U.S. dollars. The first column refers to combined nominal GDP per capita.

Table 2. Caribbean Countries: Real GDP Growth
(In percent)

	Real GDP Growth[1]					Volatility of GDP Growth[2]			
	1981–98	1981–89	1990–98	1994–98	1998	1981–98	1981–89	1990–98	1994–98
Antigua and Barbuda	8.0	9.7	3.4	3.5	3.9	4.4	4.4	3.6	4.7
The Bahamas	2.4	3.4	1.1	2.4	3.0	2.7	2.8	2.3	1.7
Barbados	1.1	1.5	0.6	4.0	4.8	3.5	3.2	4.0	0.9
Belize	6.1	5.0	5.0	2.4	1.4	4.5	5.6	3.5	1.2
Dominica	5.5	6.7	2.7	2.6	3.5	3.2	3.8	1.3	0.8
Grenada	6.5	7.0	3.7	4.5	5.8	2.5	2.1	2.4	1.8
Guyana	1.3	−2.2	6.1	5.8	−1.3	5.8	4.8	4.3	3.9
Jamaica	2.1	3.3	0.6	−0.5	−0.7	3.1	3.8	1.8	1.3
St. Kitts and Nevis	8.1	7.8	4.9	5.2	1.6	2.7	3.1	1.9	2.2
St. Lucia	8.1	9.5	3.5	2.7	2.9	3.9	4.5	1.7	1.0
St. Vincent and the Grenadines	7.4	8.5	3.6	3.2	5.2	3.2	1.2	3.7	4.2
Suriname	1.2	−0.8	3.5	7.2	3.9	6.6	5.2	7.6	7.6
Trinidad and Tobago	−0.6	−3.0	2.4	4.1	4.4	4.2	3.9	2.3	0.5

Sources: IMF, Recent Economic Developments reports; and World Economic Outlook database.
[1]Annual averages; measured as the growth rate for the period divided by the number of years considered.
[2]Measured as standard deviation of annual growth rates during each period.

Box 1. Natural Disasters in the Caribbean Region

Caribbean countries face various kinds of natural disasters, such as hurricanes, torrential rains, earthquakes, volcanic eruptions, and landslides. Given their small size, the impact of a major natural disaster can be devastating, including the loss of human lives and substantial economic damages.

According to official data (from the Organization of American States, USAID, and the Caribbean Disaster Emergency Response Agency), some recent major disasters and an indication of their impact are:

- In Jamaica, Hurricane Gilbert (1988) left over 200,000 homeless and damaged over 95 percent of all health sector facilities. Total losses exceeded 65 percent of annual GDP.

- Hurricane Hugo (1989) resulted in damages to Montserrat in excess of 200 percent of GDP.

- Flooding and landslides associated with tropical storm Debbie (1994) caused damages corresponding to 18 percent of GDP in St. Lucia.

- Hurricanes Luis and Marilyn (1995) affected a number of countries in the region. Losses totaled 65 percent of GDP in Antigua. These storms also destroyed nearly the entire banana crop in Dominica and a substantial portion of it in St. Lucia.

- Hurricane Georges (1998) destroyed 85 percent of the housing stock and 50 percent of the sugar harvest in St. Kitts and Nevis, as well as causing extensive damage to health, education, and tourism facilities; it damaged 15 percent of the livestock sector in Antigua and Barbuda.

- Hurricane Lenny (1999) put 65 percent of the island of Barbuda under water and destroyed 95 percent of its agricultural crops; it led to the closure of the major hotel and employer in Nevis, and severely damaged urban areas in St. Kitts.

- Losses from individual landslides have been smaller, but their collective impact has been substantial. Volcanoes have caused extensive damage to agricultural areas in several countries, including St. Vincent and the Grenadines, Martinique, and Montserrat.

Natural disasters have had particularly damaging effects on the agricultural and tourism sectors in the region through the destruction of crops and infrastructure (commercial and residential buildings). In addition, these disasters resulted in the cancellation and diversion of cruiseship calls. Unfortunately, insurance coverage for damages is only partial. As a result of the frequency of disasters in the region, both insurance premiums and deductibles are high. In the last decade, there have been episodes when some insurance providers decided to cease operating in the region.

Caribbean countries have developed some regional initiatives in the areas of prevention and coordination of disaster management. With the assistance of the World Bank, ongoing work includes improving risk sharing for catastrophic losses in small states, involving market arrangements to handle disaster risks for private and public sectors assets and infrastructure.[1]

[1]See World Bank (2000).

Box 2. Regional Competition and Tourism Industry in the Caribbean

Caribbean countries, such as The Bahamas, Barbados, and the U.S. Virgin Islands, are long-established tourist destinations. Even though its regional market share declined during the 1990s, The Bahamas remains (after Puerto Rico) the second largest tourist destination within the region (with 11.3 percent of the region's visitor arrivals in 1998), ahead of the Dominican Republic (9.3 percent) and Jamaica (6.5 percent). The OECS countries are relatively new destinations, where tourist arrivals grew rapidly in the 1980s and in the early 1990s. These countries received 7.7 percent of the region's total tourists in 1998.

During the 1990s, the annual increase in the number of stayover visitors to the broad Caribbean region (including countries and territories within the Caribbean Sea that are not CARICOM members) averaged 5 percent, while the annual increase in the number of cruise-ship visitors averaged 5.9 percent (Tables A5 and A6). Concurrently, hotel facilities have been expanding at a fast rate, with the number of hotel rooms increasing by 145 percent from 1990 to 1998 for the broad Caribbean region and by 78 percent for the countries considered in this paper (Table A7). English-speaking Caribbean destinations have faced increasing competition from the less expensive destinations in the region, such as Cuba and the Dominican Republic. As a result, the market share for the English-speaking countries has declined, as measured both by stayover visitors (to 29.6 percent in 1998 from 33.6 percent in 1990) and by cruise passengers arrivals (to 40 percent in 1998 from 44.2 percent in 1990).

Despite their natural comparative advantages in tourism, English-speaking Caribbean countries are generally considered expensive tourist destinations, reflecting both higher airline and accommodation prices. The region's competitiveness may suffer from uncertainties associated with frequent natural calamities, the lack of economies of scale, and relatively high costs of labor, basic services, and transportation.

While agriculture and mining remain important, the structure of production in some countries began to shift more decidedly toward services in the 1990s. In recent years, the share of agriculture and mining has declined, and the contribution of services in GDP has increased for many countries in the region, as they try to find new sources of employment and income generation (Table A2). While The Bahamas has been an offshore banking center since the 1940s, offshore financial activities have become more prevalent in nearly all the small countries in the region since the early 1980s.

The number of visitors to the Caribbean region grew in the latter half of the 1990s, but total tourist receipts did not keep pace with growth in nominal GDP. For the region as a whole, tourist receipts represented more than 35 percent of external earnings and 18 percent of GDP during 1994–98 (Table A3). For some of the larger regional tourist destinations, such as The Bahamas and Jamaica, tourist receipts have been declining as a percent of GDP since 1995, while rising slightly for Barbados. In the smaller island economies of the OECS, after a sharp increase in the 1980s, growth in tourist receipts as a percent of GDP have declined in Antigua and Barbuda and Grenada, but increased in Dominica, St. Lucia, and St. Vincent and the Grenadines. The tourism sector in some countries, particularly in Antigua and Barbuda and St. Kitts and Nevis, was adversely affected by hurricanes in 1995 and 1998. For most countries, tourism receipts have declined in importance as a source of foreign exchange earnings since the mid-1990s. However, in five countries—Guyana, Jamaica, St. Lucia, St. Vincent and the Grenadines, and Trinidad and Tobago—tourism receipts have accounted for a growing share of exports of goods and services.

During the 1990s, the tourism market share of the CARICOM member countries, relative to the broader Caribbean region, fell to 37½ percent in 1998 from 40 percent in 1990. Tourist arrivals expanded at an average annual rate of 4.5 percent for the CARICOM member countries, compared with an annual average of 5.7 percent for the broader Caribbean region. The Dutch and English-speaking Caribbean economies are facing increasing competition from their Spanish-speaking neighbors and require continuing efforts to maintain their market share (Tables A4–A7 and Box 2).

External Sector Developments

Caribbean countries have highly open economies: in 1994–98, exports plus imports of goods and nonfactor services averaged more than 96 percent of GDP for all the countries in the region. Partly as a result, the Caribbean countries are affected by cyclical economic fluctuations in North American and European countries, from which they obtain most of their foreign exchange earnings. More than 60 percent of the region's merchandise exports are sold in North American and European markets; the proportion is even higher for some smaller countries. Likewise, the United States, Canada, and the countries of the European Union (EU) account for more than 80 percent of the visitors to the region (Tables 3 and 4).

Table 3. Caribbean Countries: Stayover Tourist Arrivals by Country of Origin[1]

	1994	1995	1996	1997	1998	1994	1995	1996	1997	1998
	(In thousands)					(In percent)				
United States	2,616.0	2,708.5	2,714.0	2,741.4	2,734.4	56.2	57.0	56.2	55.8	55.7
Canada	373.8	355.9	354.8	369.8	367.6	8.0	7.5	7.4	7.5	7.5
Europe	861.3	862.0	921.8	999.4	1,014.4	18.5	18.1	19.1	20.3	20.6
United Kingdom	455.8	454.6	490.2	550.7	597.4	9.8	9.6	10.2	11.2	12.2
Germany	147.0	134.3	132.7	115.5	108.5	3.2	2.8	2.7	2.3	2.2
France	39.1	44.2	50.8	52.1	41.9	0.8	0.9	1.1	1.1	0.9
Other	219.3	228.9	248.1	281.1	266.6	4.7	4.8	5.1	5.7	5.4
Caribbean	418.5	451.8	453.4	478.3	496.2	9.0	9.5	9.4	9.7	10.1
Other	388.6	375.5	382.5	325.8	300.9	8.3	7.9	7.9	6.6	6.1
Total	4,658.2	4,753.7	4,826.5	4,914.7	4,913.5	100.0	100.0	100.0	100.0	100.0

Source: Caribbean Tourism Organization.

[1]Includes tourist arrivals to Antigua and Barbuda, The Bahamas, Barbados, Belize, Dominica, Grenada, Guyana, Jamaica, St. Kitts and Nevis, St. Lucia, St. Vincent and the Grenadines, Suriname, and Trinidad and Tobago.

Table 4. Caribbean Countries: Direction of Trade[1]
(1998, unless otherwise indicated)

	United States	United Kingdom	CARICOM	Other
	(Exports by destination, in percent of total exports)			
Barbados	40.8	17.1	34.2	7.8
Belize[2]	45.5	30.0	4.2	20.2
Dominica	5.2	25.1	58.6	11.1
Guyana[3]	24.2	18.7	8.8	48.2
Jamaica[4]	39.5	12.1	3.3	45.1
St. Kitts and Nevis[5]	18.1	22.3	5.5	54.1
St. Lucia	21.0	60.0	16.3	2.7
St. Vincent and the Grenadines	5.2	42.2	49.1	3.5
Suriname[6]	21.7	2.2	...	76.1
Trinidad and Tobago	35.3	...	29.3	35.4
	(Imports by origin, in percent of total imports)			
Barbados	30.6	7.7	15.5	46.1
Belize[2]	51.5	5.3	3.9	39.3
Dominica	38.1	13.1	24.4	24.4
Guyana	29.3	7.8	21.2	41.8
Jamaica	50.9	3.9	10.4	34.8
St. Kitts and Nevis	42.4	11.3	17.2	29.1
St. Lucia	40.0	9.2	21.2	29.6
St. Vincent and the Grenadines	39.4	12.5	24.5	23.6
Suriname[7]	24.4	1.8	13.6	60.2
Trinidad and Tobago	44.5	4.9	3.5	47.1

Source: IMF, Recent Economic Developments reports.

[1]Data not available for Antigua and Barbuda, The Bahamas, and Grenada.

[2]1997.

[3]Other export destinations include 23.5 percent to Canada.

[4]Other export destinations include 11.5 percent to Canada and 21.6 percent to other European countries.

[5]1995.

[6]Other export destinations include 47.8 percent to other European countries.

[7]Other import origins include 17.3 percent from the Netherlands.

Box 3. Preferential Trade Arrangements for Caribbean Economies

France, Italy, Portugal, Spain, and the United Kingdom have traditionally adopted preferential trading arrangements with former colonies or overseas territories. Other European countries, such as the Benelux countries, Denmark, Germany, and Ireland, have had traditionally more open market arrangements. Despite the adoption of a common external tariff, the European Economic Community, and later the 15 EU members, have agreed to maintain past preferential trade and aid facilities to the ACP group of countries under the Lomé Conventions, the first of which was signed in 1975 and the fourth one in 1990.

The conventions granted a wide range of trade preferences to the ACP countries, including duty-free access for most manufactured and agricultural commodities, and established separate protocols for Caribbean exports of bananas, sugar, beef, and rum, by assigning export quotas to the Caribbean states for these products. Since they are discriminatory and nonreciprocal, the trade preferences (and the quota system) have been subject to waivers from EU obligations under international trade agreements. To complement the trade preferences, the EU provides technical and financial assistance to the ACP countries in order to improve their competitiveness.

Preferential access to the EU for bananas has been the most publicly discussed issue, as these policies have led to a five-year trade dispute involving the United States and the EU. Following the 1997 WTO decisions requesting changes in its banana import regime, the EU issued a new council regulation in January 1998 that gives preferential treatment to ACP bananas, combining tariff and quota arrangements and cross-subsidies through import licenses. The WTO ruled in April 1999 that the EU's modified system was still in violation of world trade rules and suggested some alternatives that would maintain the EU's desire to give preferential treatment to bananas from ACP member countries, but would eliminate discriminatory quotas and cross-subsidies through the license system.

However, the effective preferences that these provisions grant to ACP countries have been gradually eroded as a consequence of the general reduction in tariff rates and trade preferences that the EU has agreed to with other developing countries. Upon the expiration of the Lomé IV Convention, and the related WTO waiver for its provisions, the renegotiation process between the EU and ACP countries has led to an agreement that calls for a progressive dismantling of the discriminatory quotas and the licensing system in accordance with WTO rules, within an eight-year transition period.

The United States also provides preferential access to most Caribbean exports through the Caribbean Basin Economic Recovery Act launched in 1983 and amended in 1990 and in May 2000, aimed at encouraging diversification of regional economies. Provisions include tariff concessions granted on a unilateral and nonreciprocal basis, subject to some discretionary conditions, on most regional exports with some exceptions, such as fuel and related products.

The U.S. Trade and Development Act, signed into law in May 2000, enlarged those provisions and restored the competitive advantages the Caribbean region enjoyed prior to the implementation of the North American Free Trade Agreement (NAFTA), which led to increased competition from Mexican products.

Merchandise exports from the Caribbean region are generally concentrated in a few commodities, namely minerals and agricultural crops. For every country in the region, its three top export commodities account for more than 60 percent of total exports (Table A8). This concentration of exports, along with exogenous shocks—such as swings in the terms of trade and natural disasters—explains a large part of the observed volatility in export earnings over the last few decades (Table A9).

Countries across the Caribbean region import goods mainly from the United States and from other CARICOM countries. The United Kingdom and the Netherlands (in the case of Suriname) are also important suppliers of imports for some countries. Consumer goods tend to represent a high proportion of imports, particularly in the OECS countries (Table A10). The share of consumer goods in total imports is less than 40 percent for only three countries: Guyana, Jamaica, and Trinidad and Tobago.

Agricultural exports of the region are characterized by high production costs and are shipped to protected markets. The EU provides preferential access to its market for a number of commodities from the African, Caribbean, and Pacific (ACP) group of countries. Caribbean countries have relied heavily on this system of preferential access, through a tariff-quota system for a number of commodities, particularly bananas (for Belize, Dominica, Grenada, Jamaica, St. Lucia, St. Vincent and the Grenadines, and Suriname) and sugar, molasses, and rum (for Belize, Guyana, Jamaica, St. Kitts and Nevis, and Trinidad and Tobago). The United States also provides preferential access for some regional exports under the Caribbean Basin Initiative (CBI) and the Trade and Development Act. The benefits available under these preferential trade regimes are nonetheless progressively being eroded (see Box 3). Despite these preferences, the importance of agricultural exports within total exports has declined in recent

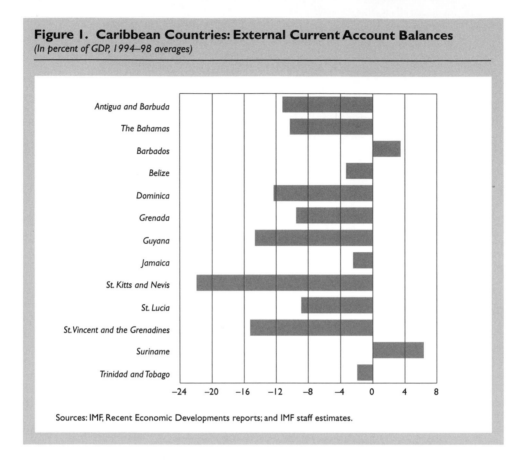

Figure 1. Caribbean Countries: External Current Account Balances
(In percent of GDP, 1994–98 averages)

Sources: IMF, Recent Economic Developments reports; and IMF staff estimates.

years for some countries in the region and the decline is likely to continue in light of the scheduled phasing-out of preferential access under the EU-ACP Partnership Agreement.

Except for Trinidad and Tobago and Suriname, countries in the region have large trade and current account deficits (Tables A11–A13), despite, in some cases, sizable current transfers associated with migrants' remittances. This is especially true for the small island economies, where exports of goods account for less than 43 percent of total exports earnings. Also, the relative share of merchandise and services within export receipts is generally skewed in favor of services, except for Belize and Jamaica where there is more balance (Table A12). Current account imbalances have occurred in recent years even in countries with traditional surpluses, such as Suriname and Trinidad and Tobago (Figure 1).

In recent years, foreign direct investment flows to the region have financed a large share of the current account deficits (Figure 2). Foreign direct investment flows have permitted countries to sustain high levels of domestic investment and have been channeled mainly to the mining and energy-based sectors in Jamaica and Trinidad and Tobago and to

the tourism sector in the smaller countries (Table A14). Since the early 1980s, increases in foreign direct investment flows have partially offset a decline in official borrowing and grants. The current account deficits of the countries in the region are also financed to some extent by commercial borrowing (Table A15). A larger share of commercial borrowing is directed to the nonbanking private sector (Table A16). This feature reflects largely international banks' financing of a few specific projects in the tourism and infrastructure sectors in the region. Official grants, though significant, have been declining. They averaged 2.2 percent of GDP in the OECS economies, and 3.6 percent in Guyana, during 1994–98. Official grants to Suriname averaged 12.4 percent of GDP over the same period, but have declined appreciably in recent years (Table A17). Since the late 1980s, Dominica, Grenada, St. Lucia, and St. Vincent and the Grenadines have been receiving STABEX grants[6]

---

[6]Grants under EU agreement are aimed to assist with economic diversification as part of adjustment to reduction in the preferential access for banana exports to the EU.

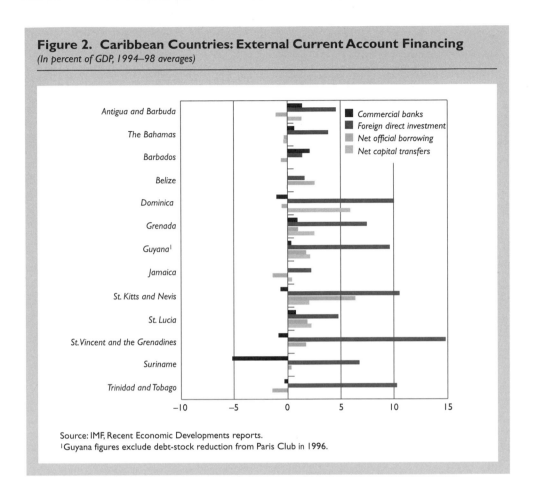

Figure 2. Caribbean Countries: External Current Account Financing
(In percent of GDP, 1994–98 averages)

Source: IMF, Recent Economic Developments reports.
[1]Guyana figures exclude debt-stock reduction from Paris Club in 1996.

from the EU that have been used increasingly for health, education, and economic diversification.

Monetary and Exchange Rate Regimes and Developments

Together with generally prudent fiscal and financial sector policies, the commitment to a fixed exchange rate (in terms of the U.S. dollar) by many of the small economies of the Caribbean has been a key factor in creating a stable macroeconomic environment and maintaining inflation close to international levels (Table 5). Following a long tradition of monetary cooperation, Antigua and Barbuda, Dominica, Grenada, St. Kitts and Nevis, St. Lucia, and St. Vincent and the Grenadines, together with two U.K. territories, Anguilla and Montserrat, established the Eastern Caribbean Central Bank (ECCB) in 1983.[7] The stability in the value of their

common currency, the Eastern Caribbean dollar, is ensured through strong backing by the ECCB's pooled official reserves. The Bahamas, Barbados, and Belize have also pegged their currencies to the U.S. dollar.[8]

In contrast, Guyana, Jamaica, and Trinidad and Tobago have floating exchange rate regimes, with their central banks undertaking discretionary currency interventions from time to time. Suriname has a dual exchange rate regime, with a large margin between the official and the parallel exchange rates; the authorities have begun to take steps toward unifying the exchange rates. In the last two decades, all of these countries have experienced episodes of economic instability, when explicit or implicit commitments on the exchange rate could

---

[7]Anguilla joined the ECCB in 1987. On the ECCB arrangement, see van Beek and others (2000).

[8]The ECCB countries use a common currency—the Eastern Caribbean dollar—and the exchange value of this currency has been fixed to the U.S. dollar at the rate of EC$2.70 = US$1 since 1976. The Bahamian dollar is fixed at parity to the U.S. dollar, while the currencies of Barbados and Belize are fixed to the U.S. dollar at a rate of 2 to 1.

Table 5. Caribbean Countries: Inflation
(Consumer price index inflation, in percentage points)[1]

	1981–85	1986–90	1991–95	1996–98
	(Countries with fixed exchange rates pegged to the U.S. dollar)			
Antigua and Barbuda	3.2	5.8	2.4	2.3
The Bahamas	5.8	6.1	3.3	1.3
Barbados	7.3	4.3	2.9	2.4
Belize	5.1	2.6	3.8	1.6
Dominica	4.8	5.0	1.8	1.9
Grenada	6.6	2.8	2.8	1.8
St. Kitts and Nevis	4.0	2.5	2.4	5.3
St. Lucia	3.3	4.3	4.5	0.9
St. Vincent and the Grenadines	4.7	4.1	2.9	2.6
Unweighted average	5.0	4.2	3.0	2.2
	(Countries with flexible exchange rates)			
Guyana	28.0	34.6	34.6	4.7
Jamaica	22.2	19.1	85.1	12.1
Suriname	8.5	30.2	1,197.6	15.2
Trinidad and Tobago	14.3	11.8	7.5	4.7
Memorandum item:				
United States	5.3	4.5	2.9	2.2

Sources: IMF, Information Notice System, and Recent Economic Developments reports.
[1]Measured as the inflation for the period divided by the number of years within the period.

not be maintained (Figure 3). Except for Suriname, countries within the region have been successful in reducing inflation to single-digit rates. Consistent with an official emphasis on inflation as the main monetary policy objective, the countries that maintain flexible exchange rates have limited the growth rates of monetary aggregates and sought to limit exchange rate depreciation, as in the cases of Jamaica and Trinidad and Tobago.

On average, the level of gross international reserves in the region has remained fairly stable, at the equivalent of about three months of imports. However, Belize, Guyana, and Jamaica have experienced a decline in coverage in the last three or four years (Table 6). In the case of the ECCB, the strict limits on credit to member governments have helped to maintain a foreign exchange cover for its demand liabilities in excess of 95 percent in recent years, compared with the 60 percent mandated in its Articles of Agreement.[9]

Within the region, there has been a general trend toward a real effective appreciation of the local currencies since mid-1995, despite fluctuations since 1998. This largely reflects the strengthening in the value of the U.S. dollar against major currencies, particularly between mid-1995 and mid-1998, and the fact that the inflation differential remains large in a few of the countries (Figures 4–6).

Real interest rates remain relatively high throughout the region (Table 7), as a result of high reserve and liquidity requirements and generally conservative monetary policies, combined in some cases with large fiscal imbalances. For some countries, the perception of exchange rate risk may also be a contributing factor. In addition, the cost of banking services in most countries in the region remains high, reflecting the lack of economies of scale, relatively undiversified loan portfolios, due to the small size of the economies, and the oligopolistic nature of the banking industry in most countries in the region.[10]

Banking intermediation in the region is relatively high compared with Latin American countries, as measured by the ratios of bank lending and deposits

---

[9]In the case of the ECCB, each member country has unrestricted access to the common reserve pool as long as it has the domestic resources to acquire them. The ECCB calculates imputed reserves for each member as the sum of currency in circulation and the net asset positions at the ECCB of the government and the commercial banks in each territory.

[10]For the OECS countries, see Randall (1998).

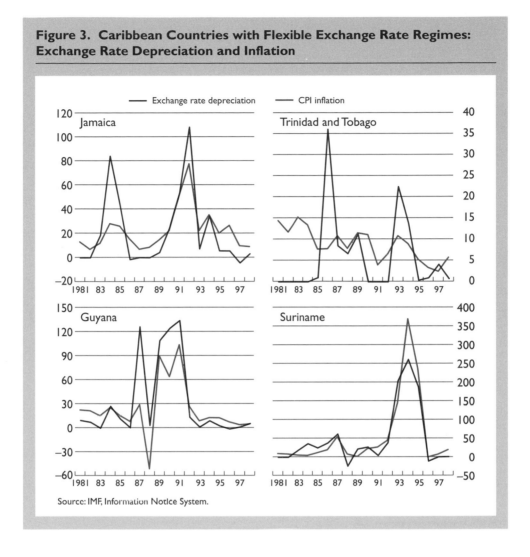

Figure 3. Caribbean Countries with Flexible Exchange Rate Regimes: Exchange Rate Depreciation and Inflation

Source: IMF, Information Notice System.

to GDP.[11] In most countries in the region, commercial banks tend to play a very large role in the financial sector, although nonbank financial institutions in many countries are becoming more important as they tend to be subject to less strict prudential regulations and supervision.[12] While bond and equity markets have become an increasingly important source of financing for governments and private firms in recent years, markets and adequate institutional arrangements have only been established in a few countries. There are a range of initiatives to es-

tablish regional financial markets—such as the ECCB's efforts to establish a securities market for its member governments—and equity market capitalization has increased in recent years (Table A18).

Except for the ECCB member countries, financial institutions in the region are subject to high and unremunerated levels of reserve requirements. These reserve requirements are generally set to levels well above those needed to protect the safety and soundness of the banking system (less than 10 percent). Also, reserve requirements are not uniform across financial institutions, instruments, or local- and foreign-currency-denominated liabilities. The reserve requirements may have remained high in many countries because of reluctance to give up an important source of financing for the public sector as government securities account for a sizable proportion of the required reserve. Furthermore, since markets are relatively undeveloped, many countries have tradi-

[11]Latin American countries may have other, more developed financial intermediation markets, but data on nonbank financial institutions are not available for most of the Caribbean countries.

[12]In many countries, nonbank financial institutions are supervised by government ministries, rather than central banks. In some countries, commercial banks have established nonbank subsidiaries to take advantage of regulatory arbitrage.

Table 6. Caribbean Countries: Gross Official Reserves

	1994	1995	1996	1997	1998
	(In months of imports of goods and nonfactor services)				
Antigua and Barbuda	1.2	1.5	1.2	1.2	1.4
The Bahamas	1.2	1.1	1.0	1.2	1.8
Barbados	2.7	2.5	3.0	2.6	2.5
Belize	1.0	1.2	1.9	1.7	1.2
Dominica	1.4	1.9	1.9	1.9	2.1
Grenada	2.8	2.9	2.4	2.5	2.2
Guyana	5.1	4.6	5.2	4.7	4.4
Jamaica	1.5	2.6	2.3	2.4	2.2
St. Kitts and Nevis	2.7	2.3	2.0	2.2	2.7
St. Lucia	1.9	1.9	1.7	1.7	2.0
St. Vincent and the Grenadines	2.2	2.1	2.0	1.8	2.1
Suriname	1.6	3.4	2.5	2.8	2.8
Trinidad and Tobago	2.6	2.0	2.8	2.6	2.7
	(In percent of broad money)				
Antigua and Barbuda	14.7	15.4	12.7	12.4	12.6
The Bahamas	9.8	9.1	8.2	8.9	11.8
Barbados	17.6	19.2	22.4	21.4	18.2
Belize	11.9	11.4	18.2	17.3	11.1
Dominica	14.2	16.8	17.0	17.0	18.3
Grenada	16.7	18.0	16.1	17.2	16.7
Guyana	97.9	76.0	80.9	71.1	66.5
Jamaica	46.4	61.6	55.5	41.1	36.9
St. Kitts and Nevis	22.0	20.6	19.1	18.5	22.1
St. Lucia	18.4	18.2	15.5	16.2	17.0
St. Vincent and the Grenadines	21.6	19.6	18.7	17.2	18.5
Suriname	89.1	81.1	49.1	50.7	37.4
Trinidad and Tobago	20.7	18.9	27.9	32.2	32.1

Sources: IMF, *International Financial Statistics*, and Recent Economic Developments reports.

tionally relied on reserve requirements as an instrument in the monetary management.

Fiscal Policy

In the 1990s, the experience of the region in reducing fiscal deficits was mixed, with deficits widening toward the end of the decade.[13] The central government deficit in the region rose to 4½ percent of GDP in 1998 from 2 percent of GDP in 1994 (Table A19).[14] Some countries, which began the decade with a relatively light debt burden, were able to strengthen or maintain a relatively strong fiscal position. Despite being buffeted by fluctuations in oil prices, Trinidad and Tobago maintained a roughly balanced budget, through tight limits on spending on goods and services and transfers. The Bahamas, Barbados, St. Lucia, and St. Vincent and the Grenadines also established a track record of moderate deficits. However, a number of other countries experienced a widening of their deficits and increased debt burdens. In Jamaica, despite the maintenance of large primary surpluses, the overall budget deficit rose sharply, owing to high real interest rates and the increase in the domestic debt burden caused by government support to rehabilitate the financial sector. In St. Kitts and Nevis, the need to upgrade infrastructure in the aftermath of Hurricane Georges increased the fiscal deficit.

Caribbean countries tend to have a high revenue/GDP ratio, which increased slightly to 26½ percent in 1998 from about 26 percent in 1994 (Table A20). In recent years, some countries have strengthened revenue collections to support a higher level of public spending or to reduce fiscal deficits. Accordingly, tax receipts relative to GDP rose in many countries.

---

[13]In this section, the regional averages are unweighted.

[14]These figures partly reflect a decline in official grants to the region to 1.8 percent of GDP in 1998, from 3.2 percent of GDP in 1994.

Figure 4. ECCB Countries: Real and Nominal Effective Exchange Rates
(Monthly index, 1990 = 100)

Source: IMF, Information Notice System.

Figure 5. The Bahamas, Barbados, and Belize: Real Effective Exchange Rates
(Monthly index, 1990 = 100)

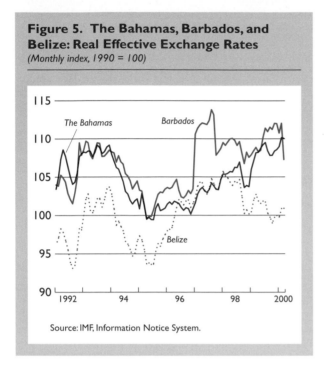

Source: IMF, Information Notice System.

Figure 6. Guyana, Jamaica, Suriname, and Trinidad and Tobago: Real Effective Exchange Rates
(Monthly index, 1990 = 100)

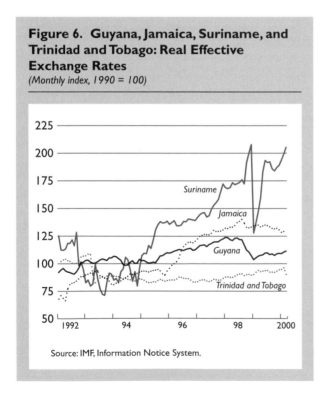

Source: IMF, Information Notice System.

For the region as a whole, reining in public expenditure has proved difficult, with some tendency for expenditures to creep upward over time. Central government expenditure rose to 33 percent of GDP in 1998 from 30 percent of GDP in 1994 (Table A21). In many countries, public sector payrolls constitute a sizable part of current expenditure and large real wage increases have been a major source of fiscal imbalances, with the average public wage bill for the region rising to about 12 percent of GDP in 1998 from 10½ percent of GDP in 1994. Part of the reason for this increase can be attributed to relatively strong trade unions and the system of public salary reviews which has built-in annual increments that are not performance based. In addition, many governments in the region have found it increasingly necessary to make supplementary wage adjustments for the civil service to retain qualified employees for critical positions—the "brain drain" being part of the problem. Also, most countries have been reluctant to reduce the size of the public sector workforce because it may exacerbate unemployment. Nevertheless, Guyana reduced the size of its public sector in the 1990s, cutting central government employment by 50 percent and public sector employment by 45 percent.

For a few countries, rising interest payments have also contributed to the observed increase in central government expenditure. For St. Kitts and Nevis, St. Lucia, and St. Vincent and Grenadines, this reflected primarily an increase in external debt. In Jamaica, it resulted from sharp growth in the stock of domestic debt, while public external debt declined (Table 8).[15] Guyana began the decade with a particularly large debt overhang but has reduced it through greater access to concessional borrowing, grants, and debt relief under the Heavily Indebted Poor Countries (HIPC) Initiative.

The region as a whole has made significant progress as regards privatization. Many countries have taken steps to privatize state-owned enterprises. They have also made efforts to improve the operating performance of enterprises that have remained within the public sector. As in other developing countries, privatization is seen as a means to improve economic efficiency, to lessen the role of the public sector, and to generate funds for the budget. The widening of the consolidated public sector deficit to 4¼ percent of GDP in 1998 from 1 percent of GDP in 1994 reflected a worsening in central government balances (Table 9). Excluding the central government, the consolidated balance of the nonfinancial public enterprises improved from approximate balance to a surplus of about 1 percent of GDP in this period. For some Caribbean countries, however, major public enterprises

---

[15]Data on domestic debt are only available for a few countries in the region.

Table 7. Caribbean Countries: Interest Rates
(In percent a year, end of period)

	1994	1995	1996	1997	1998
Antigua and Barbuda					
Treasury bills[1]	7.7	7.7	7.7	7.7	7.7
Deposits[2]	4.0–8.0	4.0–8.0	4.0–8.0	4.0–8.0	4.0–8.0
Lending[3]	10.5–12.0	10.0–11.5	10.0–12.0	10.0–12.0	10.0–13.5
The Bahamas					
Treasury bills	2.0	4.6	4.4	4.4	3.9
Deposits[2]	4.0	3.7	3.6	3.4	3.2
Lending[3]	6.8	6.8	6.8	6.8	6.8
Barbados					
Treasury bills	7.8	8.3	5.6	4.9	5.7
Deposits[2]	5.0	5.2	5.2	4.5	4.2
Lending[3]	11.0	10.9	11.1	10.6	10.4
Belize					
Treasury bills[4]	4.3	4.1	3.8	3.5	3.8
Deposit[5]	8.6	9.4	9.1	9.2	8.8
Lending[6]	14.8	15.7	16.3	16.3	16.5
Dominica					
Treasury bills	6.4	6.4	6.4	6.4	6.4
Deposits[2]	4.0–5.5	4.0–5.5	4.0–5.5	4.0–5.5	4.0–5.5
Lending[3]	9.0–10.0	9.0–10.5	9.0–10.5	9.0–10.5	9.0–10.5
Grenada					
Treasury bills	6.5	6.5	6.5	6.5	6.5
Deposit[5]	4.2	4.0	4.1	4.5	4.6
Lending[3]	10.5	10.5	10.5	10.5	10.5
Guyana					
Treasury bills	18.6	15.5	9.9	8.2	8.8
Deposits[2]	11.2	10.5	7.7	7.4	7.1
Lending[3]	19.9	19.1	17.4	16.9	16.6
Jamaica					
Treasury bills	27.0	35.0	25.2	24.6	21.3
Deposits[2]	15.0–25.0	15.0–24.0	15.0–25.8	10.3–15.0	7.0–14.0
Lending[3]	43.0	45.1	37.1	33.6	30.4
St. Kitts and Nevis					
Treasury bills	6.50	6.50	6.50	6.50	6.50
Deposits[2]	4.0–5.5	4.0–5.0	4.0–5.0	4.0–5.0	4.0–5.0
Lending[3]	10.0–13.0	9.5–13.0	9.5–13.0	9.5–12.0	9.5–13.0
St. Lucia					
Treasury bills	7.0	7.0	7.0	7.0	7.0
Deposits[2]	4.0–6.0	4.0–6.0	4.0–6.0	4.0–6.0	4.0–6.0
Lending[3]	9.0–10.0	9.5–10.0	9.5–11.0	9.5–10.5	9.5–10.5
St. Vincent and the Grenadines					
Treasury bills	6.5	6.5	6.5	6.5	6.5
Deposits[2]	4.0–5.5	4.0–6.0	4.0–5.5	4.0–5.5	4.0–5.5
Lending[3]	10.5–11.0	9.5–11.0	10.0–11.0	10.0–12.5	10.0–12.5
Suriname					
Deposits	7.5	21.0	17.8	...	...
Lending	15.4	40.2	35.8	...	...
Trinidad and Tobago					
Treasury bills	10.2	8.5	10.5	9.8	11.9
Deposits[7]	6.5	5.8	5.4	5.3	5.8
Lending[8]	16.0	15.0	15.5	15.5	17.5

Sources: IMF, Recent Economic Developments reports, and *International Financial Statistics*.

[1] Issue rate.
[2] Savings deposits.
[3] Prime rate.
[4] Treasury bill discount rate.
[5] Time deposits.
[6] Commercial loans.
[7] Weighted average.
[8] A general guiding rate set by the commercial banks and not a specific rate for prime customers.

Table 8. Caribbean Countries: Public External Debt
(In percent of GDP)

	1994	1995	1996	1997	1998
Antigua and Barbuda	81.4	89.8	84.3	78.0	65.9
The Bahamas	9.8	8.8	7.8	9.9	8.3
Barbados[1]	20.9	19.5	18.5	16.2	14.4
Belize[1]	32.7	30.3	34.9	36.4	38.9
Dominica[2]	47.6	44.1	41.7	35.0	32.7
Grenada	32.1	30.5	28.8	26.7	28.5
Guyana[3]	392.0	318.0	223.4	182.7	190.8
Jamaica[1]	80.3	68.6	50.8	49.3	48.2
St. Kitts and Nevis	21.2	22.3	23.5	37.5	39.0
St. Lucia[1]	22.7	22.8	24.8	26.4	27.0
St. Vincent and the Grenadines	36.2	33.6	52.0	51.0	52.6
Suriname	...	28.8	22.1	20.8	27.0
Trinidad and Tobago	41.7	37.6	35.2	25.9	22.9

Source: IMF, Recent Economic Developments reports.
[1]Fiscal year begins on April 1.
[2]Fiscal year begins on July 1.
[3]Before Heavily Indebted Poor Countries (HIPC) Initiative.

Table 9. Caribbean Countries: Consolidated Public Sector Balances[1]
(Overall balances after grants, in percent of GDP)

	1994	1995	1996	1997	1998
Antigua and Barbuda	−5.1	−6.5	−3.6	−7.3	−4.3
The Bahamas	0.5	−0.2	−1.6	−3.2	−2.5
Barbados	2.8	2.1	−1.8	−0.2	0.2
Belize	−5.6	−2.7	−2.1	−5.4	−5.7
Dominica	−4.4	2.3	0.5	−2.7	−2.5
Dominican Republic	−3.7	0.4	−0.5	2.1	−0.3
Grenada	−1.6	1.6	−1.3	−4.9	−5.6
Guyana	−1.1	−2.1	1.2	−3.0	−3.8
Haiti	−3.7	−4.3	−2.5	−0.5	−0.8
Jamaica	3.7	2.5	−5.7	−9.6	−12.0
St. Kitts and Nevis	0.6	1.6	−3.7	−9.7	−8.0
St. Lucia	0.5	2.1	2.2	0.9	1.1
St. Vincent and the Grenadines	−3.2	1.1	1.8	−1.7	0.3
Suriname[2]	−2.5	1.1	2.3	−5.2	−11.1
Trinidad and Tobago	3.0	1.4	0.5	−1.2	−1.6

Source: IMF, Recent Economic Developments reports.
[1]For some countries, the fiscal year begins on April 1 or July 1 (see Table 8).
[2]Central government and central bank operations.

continue to be a drain on the public finances or to be dependent on external grants. Examples include the Sugar Manufacturing Corporation in St. Kitts and Nevis and the Banana Marketing Corporation in Dominica.

The Caribbean Single Market and Economy

Caribbean countries have entered into a number of agreements to enhance their economic prospects and

---

Box 4. Evolution of CARICOM

The Caribbean Community (CARICOM) was created at the first Heads of Government Conference in Trinidad and Tobago in 1963. This conference was the first in the series of several meetings among the Commonwealth Caribbean countries that resulted in the creation of the Caribbean Free Trade Association (CARIFTA) in 1965. The Caribbean Community and CARIFTA combined to form CARICOM through the Treaty of Chaguaramas, signed in 1973. Initially there were 12 member countries: Antigua and Barbuda, Barbados, Belize, Dominica, Grenada, Guyana, Jamaica, Montserrat, St. Kitts and Nevis, St. Lucia, St. Vincent and the Grenadines, and Trinidad and Tobago. The Bahamas joined in 1983, and Suriname in 1995; Haiti still needs to complete some formalities before becoming a full member.

CARICOM has three main objectives: (1) coordination of foreign policies; (2) cooperation in common services and functional matters such as health, education, justice, culture, communications, and industrial relations; and (3) economic cooperation.

The highest decision-making organ in CARICOM, the Conference of the Heads of Government, agreed in 1989 to proceed with the formation of the Caribbean Single Market and Economy (CSME) with the launch date targeted for June 2000. This initiative aims at implementing the common market, creating a monetary and economic union, as well as raising the profile of countries in the region, especially the small member states.

There are nine amendments or Protocols—all completed—associated with the CARICOM agreement, which deal with different issues: I. Organs, institutions and procedures of the community; II. Right of establishment, the right to provide services, and the right to move capital; III. Industrial policy; IV. Trade liberalization; V. Agricultural policy; VI. Transportation policy; VII. Disadvantaged countries, regions and sectors; VIII. Disputes settlements; and IX. Rules of competition.

---

address common issues in a cooperative manner, such as the Eastern Caribbean Currency Union, the OECS, and CARICOM. In 1989, CARICOM embarked on a process of economic integration that contemplates the formation of a Caribbean Single Market and Economy (CSME), originally targeted to be launched in June 2000 (Box 4). This initiative aims at creating a single market or economy for all CARICOM countries (except The Bahamas), which will be characterized by the free movement of goods, services, capital, labor, and a common external trade policy. The single market would also entail the harmonization of internal tax regimes, the formation of a monetary union, and the adoption of a common currency.

There are three principal motives for the creation of a CSME. First, CARICOM members believe that a larger internal market will exploit economies of scale and improve the allocation of resources, leading to a higher standard of living for the region's population. Second, a CSME would increase the region's bargaining position in international negotiations and raise the profile of member countries. Third, the CSME would not only reduce barriers to trade in goods and services among member countries but also reduce barriers to trade with countries outside the common market. Regional integration will not be costless, but it has potential benefits for the members of the common market principally through effecting a more efficient allocation of resources, exploiting economies of scale, and improving productivity.

Progress toward achieving the goals of a single market economy in the Caribbean region has been slow (Table 10). The countries in the region are yet to reach the stage of a monetary union with a common currency, such as that for the OECS, and a regional capital market is still not operational. On the other hand, progress in undertaking structural reforms has generally proceeded at a faster than anticipated pace, especially in the area of trade liberalization. Also, some progress has been made toward the harmonization of domestic tax regimes.

As indicated, one area of structural reform where the region has made substantial progress is trade liberalization. Important achievements in this area were the creation in the 1970s of a common market applying to trade within the region and the elimination of most quantitative restrictions. This liberalization led to an increase in total exports of the region, particularly for nontraditional items, as well as larger intraregional trade flows. The adoption of a Common External Tariff (CET) in 1973 was the next step in the process of integrating the new common market with the rest of the world. The application of uniform tariffs to imports from outside the region, together with protocols on trade in services, were important steps toward regional integration.

To accelerate the progress in trade liberalization, CARICOM countries agreed to a schedule of phased reductions in the CET starting in 1993. The objective was to reduce in steps the maximum CET on certain goods from 45 percent to 20 percent by 1998. The less developed countries[16] were allowed

---

[16]Antigua and Barbuda, Belize, Dominica, Grenada, St. Kitts and Nevis, St. Lucia, and St. Vincent and the Grenadines.

Table 10. Status of Major Provisions of the CARICOM Single Market and Economy[1]

Initiative	Description	Status of Implementation
Free movement of goods	Free trade of goods between member states, including harmonization of standards.	Member states still have to make efforts to remove barriers to intraregional trade and the work on standards has to be more effectively administered.
Free movement of services	Free trade of services between member states.	Restrictions still exist.
Free movement of persons	Elimination of need for passports, facilitation at immigration points, elimination of need for work permits.	Travel within the region has been significantly simplified, but movement of labor is still very restricted.
Free movement of capital	Aims at convertibility of currencies with fixed exchange rates and the creation of a regional capital market.	Exchange rate controls are limited, but several currencies are floating. Capital markets are not integrated.
Fiscal coordination	Intends to harmonize internal tax regimes and incentives to industry, agriculture, and services.	Work is ongoing toward harmonization of corporate tax structures. Member states still have to agree on necessary measures for the creation of a harmonized investment environment in CARICOM.
Common external tariff	Countries have agreed to reduce their common external tariff according to a prearranged schedule.	See Table 11.

Source: CARICOM Secretariat, 1999.

[1]Haiti is in the process of becoming a full member of CARICOM and is not included in the description in the table.

to proceed at a slower pace in the reduction of import tariffs. Tariff rates imposed under the CET depend on the nature of the taxable commodity. Most commodities are grouped as competing (regional production satisfies at least 75 percent of regional demand) or noncompeting, and then each group is subdivided into inputs (primary, intermediate, and capital) and final goods. The rate structure is 0 or 5 percent on noncompeting inputs, 10 percent on competing primary and capital inputs, 15 percent on competing intermediate inputs, and 20 percent on all final goods.[17] About half of the countries in the region, accounting for the majority of its trade, have implemented the final reductions of the CET (Table 11). Some of the other countries, especially the smaller economies, have found it difficult to implement the final reductions, mainly because of the near term inability to replace lost revenues and

some concern over the ability of domestic producers to survive in a more competitive environment.

Although EU countries differ quite markedly from the Caribbean countries, several lessons can be drawn from the experience of integration within the EU. First, the process toward integration in the EU was a lengthy one. Therefore, the countries in the Caribbean should not expect a quick completion of the integration process. Second, a major difference between CARICOM and the EU is the importance of intraregional trade. Countries in the Caribbean region trade mostly with countries outside the region, while countries in the EU trade mostly with other EU countries. Hence, abstracting from other factors, the benefits from liberalizing intraregional trade are likely to be larger for the EU countries than for the countries within CARICOM, where trade links are relatively small. For CARICOM, the biggest gains are likely to be realized from liberalizing trade with countries outside the region, which is not necessarily related to the regional integration process. Third, CARICOM will need to address how the convergence process toward a single market will proceed, given the wide disparity in per capita incomes across countries in the region and the fact that countries differ markedly regarding

---

[17]The agreement on phased reductions in the CET also allows for a special higher rate on agricultural products, limited duty exemptions related to economic development, and some additional national discretion in the setting of tariff rates. In addition to tariffs, many CARICOM countries levy a customs service charge on imports at varying rates.

Table 11. CARICOM: Implementation of Scheduled Reductions in the Maximum Rate of the Common External Tariff[1]

Phases of implementation	I	II	III	IV
Period of application	Jan. 1, 1993–Dec. 31, 1994	Jan. 1, 1995–Dec. 31, 1996	Jan. 1–Dec. 31, 1997	Jan. 1, 1998 and beyond
Maximum rate	35	30	25	20
Scheduled period for implementation	Jan.–June 1993	Jan.–June 1995	Jan.–June 1997	Jan.–June 1998
Antigua and Barbuda	Completed January 2, 1995	Not implemented	Not implemented	Planned for March 2000
Barbados	Completed April 1, 1993	Completed April 1, 1995	Completed April 1, 1997	Completed April 1, 1998
Belize[2]	Not implemented	Completed April 1, 1997	Completed April 1, 1998	Planned for April 1, 2000
Dominica	Completed September 1, 1993	Completed October 1, 1995	Completed January 1, 1999	Not implemented
Grenada	Completed July 1, 1993	Completed June 30, 1995	Completed July 1, 1997	Completed January 15, 2000
Guyana	Completed January 14, 1994	Completed September 5, 1995	Completed November 1, 1997	Completed in April 30, 1999
Jamaica[3]	Completed April 1, 1993	Completed April 1, 1993	Completed January 1, 1995	Completed January, 1999
St. Kitts and Nevis	Completed July 5, 1993	Completed January 1, 1995	Not implemented	Not implemented
St. Lucia	Completed July 1, 1993	Completed July 1, 1997	Not implemented	Completed January 1, 2000
St. Vincent and the Grenadines	Completed April 2, 1993	Completed January 1, 1996	Completed January 1, 1997	Completed January 1, 1998
Suriname[4]	...	Completed January 1, 1996	Completed July 1, 1997	Planned for July 2000
Trinidad and Tobago	Completed January 1, 1993	Completed January 1, 1996	Completed January 1, 1997	Completed July 1, 1998

Sources: CARICOM Secretariat; and IMF staff.

[1]The Common External Tariff excludes agricultural products, which are subject to a rate of 40 percent. The Bahamas is a CARICOM member, but not a member of the Common Market.

[2]Belize has been granted permission to implement each phase with a two-year lag.

[3]For phase I, the maximum rate was lowered to 30 percent. For phase II, the maximum rate was lowered to 25 percent.

[4]Suriname joined the Caribbean Common Market in 1996.

their stage of development. For example, the size of fiscal deficits differs across countries in the region, and these differences are particularly sharp in some cases—for example, Trinidad and Tobago compared with Jamaica and Suriname. Also, average inflation in the OECS countries is quite low—about 2¼ percent in 1999—while inflation was 6 percent in Jamaica and 99 percent in Suriname. In these cases, issues about the speed of convergence will need to be addressed.

III   Issues Facing the Caribbean Region

The English-speaking Caribbean region has, for the most part, enjoyed economic stability, modest growth in per capita incomes, and a standard of living that compares fairly well with the rest of Latin America and the Caribbean as a whole. Also, social indicators are generally good and political systems stable. However, the increased integration of the region in the global economy has led to a number of risks that have to be addressed promptly for the countries of the region to accelerate growth and social progress in the period ahead. Although the region faces a number of issues that could be discussed, this paper concentrates on three broad topics, namely the need to: (1) lower the costs of financial intermediation and to strengthen supervision over onshore and offshore financial institutions; (2) improve the public finances—and, thereby, savings—to act as a buffer against external shocks; and (3) advance structural reforms—including further liberalization of trade—to enhance external competitiveness and promote the diversification of exports.

Monetary and Financial Sector Issues

Reserve Requirements and Monetary Policy

In some countries in the region, reserve requirements are not uniform across financial institutions and instruments, or between local- and foreign-currency-denominated liabilities. Because of the authorities' desire to encourage private capital inflows—particularly from nationals living abroad, reserve requirements are generally lower on U.S.-dollar-denominated liabilities than on domestic-currency-denominated liabilities.[18] This differential has left room for regulatory arbitrage and has contributed to:

- large intermediation spreads, with low, and sometimes negative, real deposit rates, and high real lending rates (Figure 7) and has discouraged savings and investment—particularly by lower income households and small and medium-sized businesses, which have less ability to place and seek funds abroad;

- the growth of both formal and informal nonbank financial institutions, which in most countries are subject to less comprehensive prudential supervision;

- the development of financial instruments that circumvent reserve requirements; and

- large spreads in some countries between lending rates in local currency and in U.S. dollars, which increase incentives to borrow in the latter (often from resident financial institutions), particularly in countries that also have strived to maintain a stable nominal exchange rate.

The remuneration of reserve requirements could be an interim measure toward a deeper reliance on open market operations to control liquidity. Several countries have recently either lowered reserve requirements on domestic-currency-denominated liabilities or signaled their intention to do so in the near term. They have also taken steps to harmonize reserve requirements among financial institutions and domestic-currency-denominated instruments, but have generally been reluctant to extend such harmonization of reserve requirements to U.S.-dollar-denominated liabilities.

Costs of Financial Intermediation

In many countries, the public sector continues to play a large, albeit declining, role in intermediating domestic savings through state-owned commercial and development banks, unit trusts, and actively managed social security funds.[19] Public financial in-

---

[18]The monetary authorities' limited ability to act as a lender of last resort in foreign currency and the high vulnerability of CARICOM countries to large shifts in foreign exchange inflows would suggest the elimination of the bias against domestic currency. As an alternative to reserve requirements, several countries in the region have established liquidity requirements on foreign-currency-denominated liabilities.

[19]On average, the public financial institutions account for about 40 percent of the assets of the financial sector. The social security funds for the most part are running large surpluses due to the relatively young populations and their relatively recent creation.

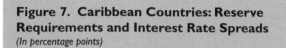

Figure 7. Caribbean Countries: Reserve Requirements and Interest Rate Spreads
(In percentage points)

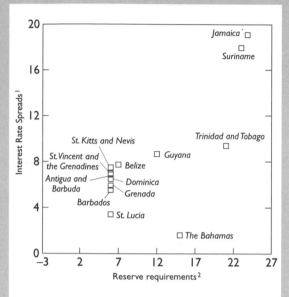

Sources: IMF, *Recent Economic Developments* reports and *International Financial Statistics*.

[1]Interest rate spread: Defined as the difference between the lending and deposit rates.

[2]Reserve requirement: Percentage of deposit liabilities required to be held with the central bank or in specified financial assets.

stitutions have been an important source of long-term financing, which private banks have for the most part been reluctant to supply for a variety of reasons including bouts of high inflation in some countries, the vulnerability of most firms to large shocks, and inadequate laws governing bankruptcy and collateral. However, public financial institutions have also reduced the efficiency—and increased the risks—of financial intermediation. Because of the use of noncommercial criteria in some cases, the concentration of loan portfolios and the ratio of non-performing loans in state-owned banks are generally higher than in their private sector counterparts. Also, the social security funds invest mainly in central government securities and state-owned banks because many countries either limit or preclude social security trust funds from investing abroad. These goals can be achieved with the privatization of state-owned financial institutions involved primarily in commercial banking and through the diversification of the investment portfolios of social security funds.

Banking systems in the Caribbean region are characterized by relatively high real interest rates, which discourage investment and growth. In some coun-

tries, this is due in part to large borrowing by the public sector, which has crowded out private sector borrowing and increased sovereign credit risk. Domestic interest rates may also reflect exchange rate risk in economies with significant exchange rate volatility. Some countries (the OECS economies, Belize, and Barbados) also have floors on deposit rates, whose elimination could facilitate a reduction in interest rates. However, in most countries, a major reason for high lending rates has been large intermediation spreads, which have been caused by:

- High reserve requirements, which are either unremunerated or remunerated at below market rates. In some countries, high liquidity requirements have created a captive market for government securities, which may have limited the return on their assets.

- High operating costs. In most countries, the banking sector is still composed of many institutions that focus primarily on their home markets with sometimes high overheads. Given the small size of these markets, most of these banks are far too small to realize economies of scale. Continued government ownership and management of large banks also contribute to the high cost structure.

- High ratios of nonperforming loans—particularly in small countries—owing in part to undiversified loan portfolios concentrated in sectors vulnerable to external shocks, delays in judicial processes, and inefficient registries for companies, properties, and deeds.[20] In addition, banks' difficulties in recovering losses by selling collateral are compounded by debtor protection laws and a reluctance, in countries with small populations and geographic areas, to purchase foreclosed property.

- Limited competition, with a handful of banks dominating lending and deposit taking in most countries. Few countries in the region have adequate anti-trust laws or enforcement agencies.

Increasing international competition, both from within and outside the region, would help to lower costs and to diversify the risks within the financial system. International foreign banks have a long history of operation in every country in the region. However, as noted in recent studies[21] the region is characterized by market segmentation and differentiation of roles among foreign, domestic, and state-owned banks. The presence of formal and informal

---

[20]See World Bank (1998).

[21]See World Bank (1998) and Randall (1998).

barriers—including discretionary restrictions on licensing and legal barriers to land holding that hamper transfer of financial assets—limit competition, maintain fragmentation, and contribute to large spread margins within the financial system. In addition, the regional development of local institutions should help to foster their diversification, both for their deposit base and lending portfolio, and for their ability to compete in international markets.

When banks and banking systems have run into difficulties in several countries in the region, depositors have generally been paid in full with public funds. In the region, only The Bahamas, Jamaica, and Trinidad and Tobago have established a formal deposit insurance system. It would be important for the countries to emphasize better education about risks associated with various investments and the lack of a de facto universal government guarantee for all depositors where insurance schemes exist.

Offshore Banking

Several governments in the region have promoted offshore financial activities as a means to reduce their economies' dependence on commodity exports and tourism. Considering the risks associated with an activity generally more leveraged than onshore banking, Caribbean countries have launched the CARICOM Bank Supervision Harmonization Project, aimed at establishing guidelines for offshore banking legislation and supervision, including minimum requirements for capital and reserves and external audits. The project also aims to promote adequate licensing policies and effective supervision and cooperation with other supervisory agencies. Nonetheless, while most governments run background checks with international enforcement agencies before granting licenses, few countries—with the exception of The Bahamas and Barbados—have adequate regulatory frameworks or fully trained staff to comprehensively supervise activities once licenses are approved. Accordingly, countries should bring the laws and regulations covering offshore activities in line with international best practices, maintain a strict firewall between offshore and onshore activities, and increase resources devoted to overseeing the offshore sector.

In order to prevent money laundering and discourage related activities, most Caribbean countries participate in the Caribbean Financial Action Task Force, which has established a process for mutual cooperation. The growth of offshore financial centers in the Caribbean region has become somewhat controversial. From the point of view of the Caribbean countries, offshore centers provide employment opportunities for the population, as well as a source of economic diversification. On the other hand, the Organization for Economic Cooperation and Development (OECD) has criticized the development of offshore centers in the Caribbean because of what is described as "harmful taxation."[22] Strengthening the legal framework under which the sector operates should be a priority, so as to avoid possible negative effects from perceptions of governance problems.

Offshore financial entities within the region are generally booking centers that serve as registries for transactions arranged and managed in other jurisdictions and they do not usually engage in financial intermediation within the region. During the 1990s, the two Caribbean offshore financial centers that report to the Bank for International Settlements (The Bahamas and the Cayman Islands) have maintained almost near-zero net cross-border positions, suggesting that they have not intermediated significant capital inflows to their host countries.[23]

Fiscal Issues

A principal goal in the Caribbean region is to raise national savings, particularly by strengthening the region's fiscal position. For many countries, an increase in public savings would enable them to finance adequate public infrastructure and social safety nets while maintaining a sound debt position and a cushion against exogenous shocks—including natural disasters.

The economic structure underlying fiscal performance in the Caribbean region has been shifting; as noted in Section II, traditional economic activities, such as agriculture, have given way to a modern service (and, to a lesser extent, manufacturing) sector. In addition, trade liberalization has led to reduced

---

[22]The OECD has issued a report on this subject titled, *Harmful Tax Competition: An Emerging Global Issue*, 1998. At the same time, the Financial Stability Forum (FSF)—created in February 1999 by the Group of Seven countries—identified in May 2000 a list of 47 "tax havens" offshore financial centers, within three categories, graded according to the quality of their financial regulation and supervision. According to the FSF terminology, the first group comprises jurisdictions generally viewed as cooperative, with a high quality of supervision, that largely adhere to international standards; the second includes countries considered to have a supervisory and cooperation framework in place, but actual performance falls below international standards, and there is substantial room for improvement; and the third comprises jurisdictions generally seen as having a low quality of supervision and/or being noncooperative with onshore supervisors, and with little or no attempt being made to adhere to international standards. Among Caribbean countries, Barbados was included in the second group, while Antigua and Barbuda, The Bahamas, Belize, St. Kitts and Nevis, St. Lucia, and St. Vincent and the Grenadines were placed in the third group.

[23]See Errico and Musalem (1999).

revenue from traditional sources, while external grants to countries in the region have shown a declining trend in recent years, placing more emphasis on revenue generation to compensate.

These developments have forced governments to seek new sources of revenue; imposed new demands on job training programs; and required increased spending on health, education, social safety nets, and infrastructure to support new industries. They have also induced governments to begin modernizing their tax and customs administrations and the management of public expenditures. Caribbean countries have thus far taken advantage of some of the easier opportunities for fiscal adjustment, such as reducing wasteful transfers and privatization. They now need to undertake fundamental reforms to improve the quality of fiscal adjustment and facilitate fiscal sustainability.

Strengthening Central Government Balances

Most countries continue to work on improving both the structure of their tax systems and its administration. For instance, both Barbados and Trinidad and Tobago successfully introduced VATs in the 1990s, replacing an existing array of indirect taxes and generating strong revenue collections. Similarly, Jamaica moved cautiously from a sales tax to the present successful general consumption tax that is akin to a VAT. Belize, which had introduced a VAT, repealed it and replaced it with a retail sales tax at a lower rate in 1999. Whatever the specific form it might take, a broad-based sales tax is an essential component of a modern tax system. Given the increasing integration of the Caribbean economies, harmonization of indirect taxes would ease administrative burdens and increase efficiency in the regional tax systems.

Customs reform has taken on particular significance in the region. These economies are very open and imports form a significant portion of the revenue base. In light of ongoing regional efforts at trade liberalization, which have resulted in a reduction in collected duties (measured as the ratio of import duties collected to the value of imports), there has been a need to reexamine the customs systems to make them more efficient in tax collection. Under the aegis of CARICOM, customs offices in most countries are adopting international standards and computerizing operations.

Several important and relatively untapped areas for strengthening revenue efforts in the region remain. One important reform would be to extend more effectively the formal system of taxation to the self-employed and the parallel economy, both of which contribute relatively little to tax revenues now. For instance, in Trinidad and Tobago, it is esti-

mated that despite a rapidly growing economy, the self-employed contribute less than 2 percent of personal income tax revenues. Although it is difficult to tax these components of the economy, it is important for efficiency and equity. In the absence of effective taxation, an excessive amount of economic activity takes place in these sectors and the formal sector's perceived inequities in bearing the burden of taxation undermine overall compliance. Sometimes presumptive or other simplified forms of tax can be used to collect revenues from these sectors of the economy.

The Caribbean tax systems include an inordinate amount of incentives for investment, particularly tax holidays and tax exemptions. These incentives weaken public revenues and require higher taxes elsewhere, distort economic activities, and impose inequitable burdens on different producers and industries. They also increase the complexity of the tax system and weaken transparency. Although Caribbean countries operate in a global environment with intense competition for investment, tax incentives encourage hit-and-run investments rather than stable, long-term investments. Moreover, studies have found that investors prefer stable political and economic environments, with high-quality public services and workforces, and a well-structured and administered tax system, with generous capital allowances.[24]

Caribbean countries could also strengthen revenues by expanding the use of property taxation, which is in place in most countries in the region even though it generally contributes little to public revenues. If efforts were made to update property ownership records and the assessed value of property, a broad-based property tax, levied at a modest rate (1 to 2 percent of property value) would provide a means to strengthen revenue sources and to gain revenues from the self-employed and parallel markets. Increased cost recovery could provide another means to raise public revenues and promote greater commercialization of the public sector.

In the smaller Caribbean nations, finding the means to finance capital spending poses a particular challenge. Infrastructure projects tend to be large and indivisible, such as building a modern airport. The geography of island nations also inevitably leads to some lack of economies of scale. Access to nonconcessional external financing markets at manageable rates is limited for many of these countries by their small size as well. In some cases (e.g., Antigua and Barbuda), ambitious public investment programs as well as guarantees for private sector liabilities or investments have led to the accumulation

---

[24]See Woodward and Rolfe (1993).

of domestic and external arrears. The use of public sector resources for the financing of big infrastructure projects could have a large, permanent impact on fiscal expenditures if it is not accompanied by cost recovery measures in the delivery of public services. At the same time, the application of strict priorities and more stringent economic criteria for the selection of investment projects is essential to maintaining a strong fiscal position.

Strengthening of Overall Public Sector Balances

Transfers to loss-making public entities continue to absorb a significant though declining part of public expenditures. Many of the countries have found it difficult to restructure, close down, or privatize loss-making public entities, particularly in the agricultural sector. The loss of protected markets for agricultural goods, such as bananas and sugar, remains a principal concern in countries where these crops comprise a significant share of exports. The concern over the loss of jobs for workers who would be difficult to retrain has stymied meaningful reform in some cases. Nevertheless, public funds are better spent on programs that address the education and skill deficiencies of such workers, rather than on propping up the enterprises. And, divestment and restructuring of these enterprises may unleash a significantly higher level of worker productivity. Moreover, the deficits of these enterprises and other entities—such as banks, utilities, and statutory bodies—have often been financed by transfers through state-controlled banks or financial institutions, which gives rise to a loss of transparency in fiscal operations. The channeling of credit to loss-making enterprises that do not reform diverts scarce funds from more productive uses.

The current financial situation of social security systems in the region tends to be strong, owing to their relatively recent establishment, a young population, and conservatism in the level of benefits paid out. However, in a number of countries, governments have tended to use the surpluses of social security funds to finance current expenditure. With aging of the population and demands for a higher level of benefits to be paid to the elderly, the social security systems are likely to confront increased financial strains. It is thus essential that efforts be made to improve their underlying financial structure, perhaps through reforms such as those in some countries in Latin America to introduce more private sector elements into the public system. Also, efforts should be made to improve the investment performance of the funds and enforcing greater compliance. In this regard, the continuing development of

financial markets in the region increases the possibilities for reforming social security systems.

Fiscal Harmonization

Caribbean countries have been successful in some forms of integration, for instance, in the formation of CARICOM in the 1970s, and in trade liberalization through the adoption of a CET and reductions in maximum tariff rates. In addition, several countries have adopted VATs in recent years, at a standard rate of 15 percent, and some harmonization of excise taxes has also occurred as part of overall trade reform. There has been less progress, however, in general fiscal harmonization, even among the smaller countries of the OECS. The challenge facing the region is to agree on a coordinated process and timing to reach common fiscal targets across countries.

Structural Policy Issues

This section considers three important structural policy issues that countries in the region will need to address in the period ahead: pursuing further trade liberalization, enhancing external competitiveness, and diversifying the structure of exports.

Effects of Trade Liberalization

Initial trade liberalization steps have been accompanied by an increase in CARICOM trade flows. The decline in the CET started in 1993 would be expected mainly to have increased imports from countries outside the region and—as trade liberalization leads to a more efficient allocation of resources—also exports. Imports (as percent of GDP) by CARICOM countries—both from other CARICOM countries and from countries outside the region—have increased in the period following the initiation of the cuts in the CET. Although total exports from the region have also grown following liberalization, they have not increased as rapidly as imports. A major factor constraining the growth of CARICOM exports has been the decline in the production of commodity exports since 1994, particularly bananas from OECS countries, which resulted from bad weather and the loss of preferential markets (Table 12).

Export composition for the region has been changing. The exportable sectors have expanded, with tourism and information services growing to 42 percent of GDP by 1998 from about 39 percent of GDP in 1994. However, some sectors have contracted because of greater competition from producers outside the region and from trade agreements elsewhere in the Western Hemisphere such as NAFTA, which extended trade preferences to Mexico. This problem

Table 12. CARICOM: Trade Flows
(In percent of GDP)

	1993	Average 1996–97	1997
CARICOM exports outside the region[1,2]	21.5	22.9	22.4
Of which:			
OECS exports outside the region[3,4]	14.7	9.3	9.1
CARICOM imports from outside the region[1,2]	37.0	42.5	45.5
Of which:			
OECS imports from outside the region[3,4]	43.1	42.6	43.2
Memorandum items:			
Intra-CARICOM trade flows[2]	3.6	4.5	4.6
OECS exports to CARICOM[4]	5.3	4.2	4.4
OECS imports from CARICOM[4]	12.7	12.9	13.1

Sources: CARICOM Secretariat; and IMF staff estimates.

[1]Excludes data on Antigua and Barbuda, The Bahamas, Haiti, and Suriname.

[2]As a percent of CARICOM GDP.

[3]OECS members are Antigua and Barbuda, Dominica, Grenada, Montserrat, St. Lucia, St. Kitts and Nevis, St. Vincent and the Grenadines, Anguilla, and the British Virgin Islands.

[4]As a percent of OECS GDP.

was addressed in May 2000 by passage of the Trade and Development Act in the United States, designed to grant trade privileges to Africa and the Caribbean. An example is the garment industry, which expanded rapidly in the 1980s but started contracting in the 1990s as trade liberalization intensified.

Trade liberalization raised consumer welfare by reducing prices of imported goods. Apart from allowing a wider variety of goods to became available for consumers, indications are that imported goods were available at lower prices with the reduction of the CET, even in cases where measures were adopted to compensate for the loss of fiscal revenues. This is particularly relevant as import content of the consumer baskets in all of the Caribbean countries is very high—ranging from about 50 percent in Jamaica to over 80 percent in St. Kitts and Nevis.

Trade liberalization has been associated with greater overall investment in the region. Although varying across countries, total investment rose to 28½ percent of GDP in 1998 from 26½ percent of GDP in 1994. Foreign direct investment increased to 6½ percent of GDP from 4½ percent of GDP during the same period. The reduction in tariffs helped reduce costs for capital and intermediate goods, crucial to the expansion in the manufacturing sector in the relatively larger economies of Barbados, Jamaica, and Trinidad and Tobago. But, also, the favorable change in relative prices for tradables brought about by liberalization has spotlighted niche areas that became competitive, such as ecotourism.

As international trade taxes—such as customs duties and service charges—are major sources of revenues for most CARICOM countries, the effect of reductions in tariffs on revenue is an important issue that needs to be given careful consideration. In general, a reduction in nominal tariff rates would be expected to lead to a loss in tariff revenue. However, increases in import volume in response to trade liberalization may mitigate such losses. Also, a reduction in tariffs—if it is large enough—may lead to increases in import value as importers are less likely to seek exemptions and special treatment, or to evade taxes through intentional misclassification, undervaluation, and outright smuggling. As indicated earlier, in the case of the Caribbean countries, it appears as if the positive effect on revenues from the increase in import volume resulting from the tariff cuts has not outweighed the negative revenue effect from the reduction in price. The overall ratio of import duties to the value of imports, as measured by the collected tariff, was reduced to 6¾ percent by 1998 from about 8¾ percent in 1994. Tariff revenue (as a percent of GDP) fell to 4½ percent from about 4¾ percent, even though imports relative to GDP rose to 46 percent from about 41 percent.

Improving Competitiveness

One common issue that most of the Caribbean countries need to address is how to improve competitiveness, given the importance of trade and tourism for the region. By improving competitiveness, countries in the region can accelerate economic growth and enhance employment opportunities. Table A9 presents a number of indicators of export performance across countries in the Caribbean region and these show that the ratio of exports of goods to GDP has been stagnant or declining between 1992 and 1998 for nearly all countries, except for The Bahamas and Barbados. For Trinidad and Tobago, the ratio of exports to GDP rose between 1992 and 1995, but declined thereafter. Similar trends are present in the data for a broader measure of export performance—the ratio of exports of goods and nonfactor services to GDP—which includes tourism. For nearly all countries in the region, this ratio has also been flat or declining except for Barbados and Dominica.[25]

Several factors bear on the fairly weak export performance of countries in the region. First, a number of countries—including Antigua and Barbuda, Guyana, Jamaica, St. Lucia, St. Vincent and the Grenadines, and Suriname—experienced adverse terms of trade shocks that more than outweighed increases in export volumes. Declines in the prices of traditional exports, for example, bananas, were the principal reason for the deteriorating terms of trade. Second, following a general pattern of depreciation between 1992 and 1995, there has been a clear trend appreciation of the real effective exchange rates for the currencies in the region since mid-1995.[26] One likely reason for this development is the decline in inflation in the United States, which is the main trading partner for nearly all of the Caribbean countries. For those countries pegged to the U.S. dollar, this pattern reflects also the strengthening of the value of the U.S. dollar against other major currencies.

For all Caribbean countries, but especially those that maintain a fixed nominal exchange rate, a way to enhance competitiveness is to restrain the increase in production costs, particularly labor costs (see Box 5). It is crucial that labor costs be kept in line with productivity for favorable future decisions about investment. As already noted, public sector wage bills have grown fairly rapidly in recent years and this trend needs to be reversed as an important first step in improving competitiveness.

In many Caribbean countries, labor market flexibility should be enhanced to solicit the appropriate labor input in economic activities. In this regard, the role of minimum wages and labor regulations may need to be reexamined. Structural policies that would help reduce production costs and enhance wage and price flexibility would be helpful in this respect. Simultaneously, other approaches to enhancing competitiveness could include raising labor productivity by encouraging the workforce to accumulate more human capital, through greater education and training.

As the tourism sector is a principal source of foreign exchange earnings for many countries in the Caribbean region, enhancing the competitiveness of this sector should be of prime importance. To avoid losing market share to other destinations, tourism development in the English-speaking Caribbean countries requires an expansion in the quantity and quality of hotels and tourism facilities, the relaxation of seasonal capacity constraints, the improvement of infrastructure, and more air access. Accordingly, and in addition to private sector efforts, the region's governments will need to increase investment in these areas to lay the foundation for expansion of the tourism sector in the medium term. Many countries have already launched initiatives of this type (expanding airport and port facilities and improving roads and utilities), as well as increasing marketing and promotional activities.

Diversification of the Economic Base

Several factors explain the relatively high degree of concentration of activity in certain sectors across Caribbean countries. First, all countries in the region are small, open economies. If there are one or two profitable sectors, they easily become very important even if they are marginal in the world economy. The lack of economies of scale in small countries tends to limit the development of some industries. Second, the production structure of many Caribbean countries tends to be highly concentrated in a few activities based on their natural resource endowments: alumina in Guyana, Jamaica, and Suriname; and petroleum and natural gas in Trinidad and Tobago. A third factor encouraging concentration of exports is the system of preferential access for certain products to the EU that was put in place as a form of economic assistance from which many countries in the Caribbean region have availed themselves. This preferential access has helped to perpetuate the relatively undiversified structure of the economies of the Caribbean.

The lack of a diversified export structure can have destabilizing effects on the economies of the Caribbean region. For economies in which exports

---

[25]The ratio of exports of goods and nonfactor services to GDP for Trinidad and Tobago rose in 1992–95, but declined in 1996–98. St. Vincent and the Grenadines experienced an increase in the ratio of exports of goods and nonfactor services in 1995–96, but it declined thereafter.

[26]Three of these countries also experienced declines in the relative price of tradables to nontradables: Jamaica over the period 1996–98; St. Kitts and Nevis during 1993–97; and Trinidad and Tobago over 1997–98.

Box 5. Public Sector Wage Levels in OECS Countries

In small open economies with fixed exchange rates, wage levels are an important determinant of external competitiveness. This is particularly the case when an economy's primary sources of foreign exchange are based on industries—such as tourism, agriculture, and light manufacturing—where labor costs dominate other operational expenses. Rising wage levels in such industries, in excess of productivity gains, will erode the cost advantage of the products and services that are generating foreign exchange and, if extended over time, with serious adverse effects on the country's balance of payments.

Among the OECS member countries, the government typically employs a significant amount of the labor force. As these countries are members of a currency union, the government should be cognizant of two factors in setting public sector wages. First, public sector salary levels, as well as their regular increments, should be formed with a view to ensuring that wage growth does not compromise the country's ability to earn foreign exchange. Second, close attention should be given to wage setting in the neighboring countries, as the flow of labor among the countries that comprise the currency union are not negligible.

Against this background, the actual pattern of public sector wages in the OECS was reviewed (based on country and ECCB data) by focusing on comparable posts in the public sectors of the eight countries. Ten occupational groupings were chosen, representing those jobs with the largest number of workers, and which together account for the majority of government employees in the OECS region. For most of these occu-

pational groupings, a mid-point salary was obtained by averaging the low and high salary level identified for each post. For the purposes of comparing purchasing-power-adjusted salary levels, price *levels* in the region were also reviewed. Price data were employed to deflate the nominal salary levels, providing an index of real wages for the 10 representative posts in the public sector. The main findings were as follows:

- There is considerable variation in nominal salary levels among OECS countries, with the country having the highest average nominal salary (St. Kitts and Nevis) paying 33 percent more than the country with the lowest average nominal salary (Grenada). The differences between specific salaries in the highest and lowest paying countries are even larger, reaching as much as 53 percent, for certain occupational groupings.

- There are surprisingly large differences in price levels across countries. Taking an unweighted average of prices, St. Kitts and Nevis has the lowest price level in the region (index = 100), with Antigua and Barbuda having the highest (index = 174).

- The compression of salary levels is greatest in Anguilla, where the salaries of the highest paid public servants are only three times those of the lowest paid. On the other hand, in St. Lucia, the salary of the highest is more than six times that of the lowest paid public servants.

---

are concentrated in a few products, a decline in the price of a principal export commodity would likely result in a deterioration in the trade balance and a decline in output, which would lead to a corresponding reduction in employment. The fiscal position also would worsen as a result of the downturn in economic activity. An increase in the price of a major export could also engender "Dutch Disease" effects,[27] which include real exchange rate appreciation, inflation, and a contraction in the output of the nonbooming tradable sectors.

Achieving greater diversification in the structure of the Caribbean economies is a major challenge. Some of the economies in the region have had limited success in reducing their dependence on a single commodity. Several countries, including Dominica, Grenada, St. Lucia, and St. Vincent and the Grenadines have achieved some success in expand-

ing their tourism sectors to compensate for the loss in banana earnings. In general, countries in the region have seen their service sectors grow during the 1990s, while the size of their traditional agricultural sectors has declined. However, governments should avoid attempts at "bad" diversification—encouraging production and export of goods for which the country does not have a comparative advantage—through subsidies or other incentives that could compromise the country's fiscal situation and lower aggregate welfare.

Strengthening fiscal positions, as well as developing consumption smoothing devices, are prudent approaches to deal with the lack of export diversification. Increased public savings could provide a buffer to limit the negative impact of exogenous shocks on domestic activity. The development of fiscal revenue stabilization funds for key export commodities could prove useful in this regard. The creation of such a fund would require that governments increase their savings and avoid using this fund to finance expenditure.

---

[27]See Neary and van Wijnbergen (1986). Trinidad and Tobago is an example of a country that experienced the Dutch Disease in the early 1980s when the price of petroleum increased sharply.

IV Economic Outlook for the Region

Despite the numerous challenges and uncertainties facing the economies of the Caribbean region in the period ahead, the economic prospects for the region as a whole appear relatively favorable (Table 13). Economic growth in the region is expected to accelerate over the medium term, averaging about 3½ percent a year over the period 2000–2005, which is significantly better than the performance of the region in the 1980s and 1990s, but below the projected average annual growth in the world economy of more than 4 percent. This acceleration in economic activity in the region is influenced by many factors, including the turnaround in economic performance in the region's export markets other than the United States, increases in the prices of the region's major export commodities, and the impact of new investment projects in the energy and tourism sectors in some countries. In the OECS countries, growth is expected to remain fairly robust, as a number of countries are pursuing—and plan to pursue—aggressive diversification strategies that encourage the expansion of service sectors. Economic growth in these countries is expected to accelerate to more than 4 percent a year on average over the medium term, which is faster than the average annual growth they enjoyed in the last decade. Nonetheless, economic growth will not likely be sufficient to reduce substantially the incidence of poverty or unemployment in the region.

Assuming no terms of trade shocks (with relatively stable oil prices) and generally prudent monetary policies, inflation in the region is projected to average about 4 percent a year over the medium term, which is above the average annual forecast for inflation in the major trading partner countries of about 2½ percent. However, over the medium term, the inflation differential between the Caribbean region and its trading partners is expected to narrow to only 0.6 percentage point in 2005 from about 1.8 percentage points in 2000. Inflation in the OECS countries is expected to fall below 2 percent.

The overall fiscal position of the region could improve over the medium term, as a number of countries take measures to strengthen the public finances. The fiscal improvements are largely dependent on the acceleration of economic growth and expenditure restraint that includes careful management of the size of the public sector workforce and restrained public sector wage increases. In addition, countries in the region are expected to see an improvement in their revenue collections as a result of past reforms to their tax systems that will yield efficiency gains over the medium term.

The external position of the Caribbean countries is projected to strengthen over the medium term. The size of the current account deficits is expected to revert to about the levels observed in the early 1990s. The decline in current account deficits stem partly from the projected increases in the prices of the region's major export commodities and the expectation of fairly robust growth in tourism receipts, as non-U.S. growth picks up. Also, the region's external competitiveness is expected to improve with the narrowing of the inflation differential with the major trading partner countries. The current account deficits of the OECS countries, while remaining much higher than the deficits of the other Caribbean countries, will also likely decline. The anticipated fiscal consolidation over the medium term will also help improve the outlook for the region's exports and external current account.

On the whole, prospects for the Caribbean region remain broadly satisfactory, but there are a number of risks to the outlook. First, economic growth in the United States—the major trading partner—has been stronger than anticipated in recent years. If the U.S. economy slows precipitously in the near term (especially in light of recent efforts to contain inflation), then growth in foreign exchange earnings for countries in the region will certainly be jeopardized, which would also adversely affect the region's growth and fiscal performance. Second, the prospects for the countries in the region depend importantly on the behavior of commodity and import prices over the medium term. In 1998 and 1999, world commodity and import prices (other than for petroleum) declined markedly, which was an important factor in keeping inflation low in

Table 13. Caribbean Region: Medium-Term Macroeconomic Projections

| | Averages | | | | | | | | | | |
	1980–89	1990–99	1997	1998	1999	2000	2001	2002	2003	2004	2005
Real GDP growth (in percent)											
CARICOM	3.0	2.6	2.2	2.3	3.8	3.6	3.4	3.4	3.5	3.6	3.6
CARICOM, excluding Jamaica and											
Trinidad and Tobago	4.2	2.9	4.0	2.7	3.8	3.5	3.3	3.4	3.6	3.8	3.8
OECS	6.4	3.4	3.5	4.0	3.7	4.7	4.2	4.1	4.2	4.2	4.2
CPI inflation (in percent)											
CARICOM	12.5	14.4	4.7	5.7	5.1	4.3	4.2	3.9	3.5	3.2	3.1
CARICOM, excluding Jamaica and											
Trinidad and Tobago	10.0	11.9	2.8	4.4	5.2	4.2	3.8	3.4	3.2	3.2	3.2
OECS	6.1	3.0	1.7	2.5	1.6	1.8	1.8	1.9	1.9	1.9	1.9
General government balance (in percent of GDP)[1]											
CARICOM	−6.9	−1.7	−4.4	−5.6	−4.3	−2.8	−2.3	−1.8	−1.1	−0.5	−0.6
CARICOM, excluding Jamaica and											
Trinidad and Tobago	−9.0	−2.8	−3.2	−3.3	−2.6	−1.7	−0.8	−0.3	0.0	0.2	0.4
OECS	−2.0	−0.8	−2.5	−2.3	−3.1	−1.2	0.0	0.5	0.9	1.0	1.3
Central government balance (in percent of GDP)											
CARICOM	−7.1	−1.9	−2.6	−3.9	−4.2	−2.7	−2.0	−1.4	−1.0	−0.6	−0.3
CARICOM, excluding Jamaica and											
Trinidad and Tobago	−8.5	−3.4	−1.5	−3.6	−3.7	−2.5	−2.4	−1.7	−1.3	−1.1	−0.8
OECS	−5.2	−2.2	−1.5	−3.7	−3.7	−1.3	−3.7	−2.6	−2.4	−2.1	−2.0
Current account balance (in percent of GDP)											
CARICOM	−5.8	−3.7	−9.0	−9.7	−7.6	−4.6	−3.7	−3.4	−3.3	−3.1	−3.1
CARICOM, excluding Jamaica and											
Trinidad and Tobago	−7.2	−6.0	−10.6	−13.5	−10.2	−7.0	−5.7	−5.2	−4.8	−4.6	−4.4
OECS	−15.0	−12.7	−13.8	−12.5	−15.7	−13.2	−11.2	−10.7	−10.2	−10.1	−9.9

Sources: IMF, *World Economic Outlook*, May 2000.
[1]Data in the 1980s available for the period 1984–89 only.

many countries in the region. If prices for imported food items were to rise more rapidly than envisaged, then inflation for the Caribbean region would likely accelerate, owing to the high import content of the consumption basket. Alternatively, higher prices for the region's main commodity exports other than petroleum—bananas, sugar, and minerals—would improve the external position of the region. If the price of oil were to rise sharply, then the external position of most countries in the region would tend to worsen, given that they are net importers of petroleum, while one country—Trinidad and Tobago—would likely experience an improvement in its external position.

V   Conclusions

Caribbean countries have attained some successes in the 1980s and 1990s in reforming their economies. On the whole, economic performance has been broadly satisfactory, but not sufficient to make serious inroads toward eliminating the problems of unemployment and poverty. These countries will face tougher challenges in the future, as their trade preferences will likely be eroded further and concessional assistance will become increasingly more difficult to attract. Also, because of their small size and their location, they remain vulnerable to external shocks, such as hurricanes, that can destroy infrastructure and income-generating activities on which they rely for sustenance.

In light of the challenges ahead, Caribbean countries will need to intensify their efforts in a number of areas. They should preserve their accomplishments in maintaining low inflation rates, but face the task of ensuring tight monetary policies while reducing high reserve requirements, so as to help reduce interest rate spreads. At the same time, they will need to find ways to deepen financial markets and improve banking sector efficiency, thus reducing the costs of financial intermediation. For that purpose, some measures should be considered, such as privatizing state-owned financial institutions, reducing barriers to entry to the financial system, and strengthening further supervision for onshore and offshore banks.

In the fiscal area, public sector deficits have tended to become larger in recent years and countries will need to address this problem more vigorously to raise public savings and investment. Reducing public sector deficits will require a balanced combination of tax reform and expenditure restraint. On the tax side, those countries that have not implemented a VAT should adopt one, given the improvement in tax performance realized by those countries that have introduced it, along with other tax reforms that improve efficiency, reduce compliance costs, and broaden the tax base. On the expenditure side, countries will need to face the difficult task of containing the growth of the public sector wage bill, while at the same time making public service sufficiently attractive to retain highly qualified employees.

Caribbean countries have generally had some success in undertaking structural reforms in the 1990s, such as the privatization of state enterprises, liberalization of trade, and removal of price controls. However, more needs to be done to position them to address the challenges in the near future. Further progress in liberalizing trade could help countries to fully enjoy the benefits of freer, more open trade. Despite the benefits from trade liberalization, certain sectors may contract when protection is removed, and countries should therefore find ways to mitigate the short-run adjustment costs that arise from liberalization. Also, the reduction of import tariffs may tend to reduce tax revenue, so an additional challenge will be to find ways to replace the lost revenue.

Given the highly open nature of the Caribbean economies and their relatively weak export performance in recent years, improving external competitiveness and diversifying the structure of their exports are key challenges in the period ahead. Competitiveness can be improved by enhancing labor productivity—through additional training and education—and by keeping wage increases, particularly in the public sector, in line with productivity growth. Furthermore, many of the economies in the region need to diversify the structure of their exports to become less reliant on earnings from a narrow group of products. This is a difficult task that cannot be achieved in a short period of time, but can be addressed through making the economy more resilient to shocks—for example, by removing administered prices and allowing market forces to operate and reallocate resources across sectors (including in the labor market).

On the whole, the economic prospects for the region are generally satisfactory over the medium term, but the projections depend importantly on the resolve of governments to pursue appropriate policies, as well as favorable developments in the rest of the world. The relatively favorable outlook for the region is not without risks, such as a slowdown in growth in the major trading partner countries or a terms of trade shock.

Statistical Appendix

Table A1. Caribbean Countries: GDP by Sector of Origin at Current Prices
(In percent of GDP, 1998 unless otherwise indicated)

	Agriculture	Mining and Quarrying[1]	Manufacturing	Construction	Wholesale and Retail Trade[2]	Hotels and Restaurants	Transport and Communication	Financial Services	Government Services	Other[3]
Antigua and Barbuda[4]	4.0	1.7	2.3	11.8	10.8	12.2	20.6	...	17.6	19.0
Barbados[4]	5.6	1.0	9.8	7.8	20.2	15.0	8.1	...	12.1	20.4
Belize[5]	22.3	0.7	16.7	5.8	16.9	...	14.4	4.7	7.4	11.1
Dominica[4]	20.2	0.9	8.8	7.8	11.3	2.6	16.7	10.7	18.8	2.2
Grenada[6]	9.5	0.5	7.0	7.3	12.1	7.9	24.5	...	16.5	14.6
Guyana	35.6	16.0	9.8	5.3	4.5		6.7	3.3	13.3	5.5
Jamaica[4]	8.0	4.9	15.1	11.4	23.0	2.0	11.8	7.6	12.7	3.5
St. Kitts and Nevis[5]	5.1	0.3	10.1	12.2	14.9	9.7	15.7	...	17.6	14.4
St. Lucia[5]	8.6	0.5	6.6	7.5	13.6	12.4	17.5	...	14.6	18.7
St. Vincent and the Grenadines[4]	9.2	0.3	5.8	11.9	13.2	1.8	17.4	6.4	15.2	18.8
Suriname	8.1	4.6	10.4	6.8	16.4	...	9.7	16.2	25.2	2.6
Trinidad and Tobago	2.2	19.7	8.3	9.8	16.7	1.2	9.4	14.7	9.4	8.6

Source: IMF, Recent Economic Developments reports.

[1]Includes petroleum sector (crude oil, refining, service, marketing, asphalt, and petrochemicals) for Trinidad and Tobago.

[2]Includes hotels and restaurants for Belize and Suriname.

[3]Includes financial services for Barbados, and hotels and restaurants for Guyana.

[4]Preliminary.

[5]Preliminary 1997.

[6]1997.

Table A2. Caribbean Countries: GDP by Sector of Origin
(In current prices, percent of GDP)

	Agriculture and Mining		Manufacture and Construction		Trade, Transportation, Tourism, and Financial Services		Government Services	
	1994	1998	1994	1998	1994	1998	1994	1998
Antigua and Barbuda[1]	5.2	5.7	11.6	14.1	52.6	43.6	16.9	17.6
Barbados[1]	7.2	6.6	15.9	17.6	42.7	43.3	13.4	12.1
Belize[2]	20.2	23.0	25.0	22.5	36.8	36.0	8.1	7.4
Dominica[1]	22.5	21.1	15.4	16.6	41.7	41.3	19.6	18.8
Grenada[3]	12.3	10.0	13.9	14.4	50.3	44.5	18.1	16.5
Guyana	58.5	51.6	15.2	15.1	12.9	14.5	8.1	13.3
Jamaica[1]	16.1	12.9	30.2	26.5	44.9	44.4	8.1	12.7
St. Kitts and Nevis[2]	6.1	5.4	21.2	22.3	50.6	40.3	19.3	17.6
St. Lucia[2]	10.4	9.1	14.8	14.1	53.0	43.5	14.2	14.6
St. Vincent and the Grenadines[1]	9.7	9.5	17.6	17.7	39.0	38.8	14.9	15.2
Suriname	26.2	12.7	22.1	17.2	32.7	42.3	9.2	25.2
Trinidad and Tobago	32.1	21.9	15.4	18.1	34.8	42.0	10.1	9.4
Weighted average	21.8	16.2	20.7	20.7	39.6	41.8	10.5	12.3

Source: IMF, Recent Economic Developments reports.

[1]Preliminary.

[2]Preliminary 1997.

[3]1997.

Table A3. Caribbean Countries: Gross Tourist Receipts

	1994	1995	1996	1997	1998	Average
(In percent of GDP)						
Antigua and Barbuda	63.9	53.9	48.5	49.5	46.7	52.5
The Bahamas	29.1	32.5	30.9	29.6	27.5	29.9
Barbados	34.6	35.8	34.7	36.3	38.4	36.0
Belize	12.9	13.1	9.1	11.2	11.4	11.6
Dominica	17.4	18.5	19.6	20.7	18.0	18.8
Grenada	31.1	32.4	31.8	30.5	28.7	30.9
Guyana	6.3	5.3	4.8	14.9	15.0	9.3
Jamaica	21.0	22.4	17.7	16.6	17.6	19.1
St. Kitts and Nevis	45.9	28.9	30.6	31.9	32.7	34.0
St. Lucia	40.0	40.9	41.6	43.6	45.4	42.3
St. Vincent and the Grenadines	18.2	20.0	23.0	24.1	23.4	21.7
Suriname	3.0	3.8	1.8	1.0	0.2	2.0
Trinidad and Tobago	1.8	1.4	1.9	3.3	3.3	2.3
(In percent of exports of goods and nonfactor services)						
Antigua and Barbuda	67.9	62.4	63.5	63.2	63.5	64.1
The Bahamas	66.4	64.1	63.4	62.7	59.1	63.1
Barbados	60.0	57.7	55.5	55.5	57.3	57.2
Belize	24.9	26.3	18.6	21.3	23.1	22.9
Dominica	35.3	37.2	37.5	36.2	31.9	35.6
Grenada	62.1	65.6	62.7	60.1	59.9	62.1
Guyana	6.0	5.2	4.7	15.1	15.6	9.3
Jamaica	34.5	31.6	33.7	32.9	36.3	33.8
St. Kitts and Nevis	60.6	53.4	52.7	49.7	51.7	53.6
St. Lucia	60.0	59.7	63.2	67.0	69.1	63.8
St. Vincent and the Grenadines	39.1	38.8	44.0	49.6	46.4	43.6
Suriname	2.6	3.7	2.6	1.4	0.5	2.2
Trinidad and Tobago	3.8	2.5	3.6	6.2	6.8	4.6

Sources: IMF, Recent Economic Developments reports; and IMF staff estimates.

Table A4. Caribbean Countries: Stayover and Cruise Tourist Arrivals
(In thousands)

	1990	1991	1992	1993	1994	1995	1996	1997	1998
Caribbean total	19,924	21,084	22,096	23,296	24,311	24,545	25,931	28,127	29,005
Independent member countries of CARICOM	8,009	8,696	9,183	9,473	9,643	9,689	10,082	10,587	10,880
Antigua and Barbuda	433	460	468	488	499	447	499	526	570
The Bahamas	3,416	3,447	3,538	3,536	3,322	3,142	3,320	3,369	3,270
Barbados	795	766	785	825	885	927	957	990	1,019
Belize	221	216	249	285	328	329	349	307	302
Dominica	52	111	137	140	182	195	257	295	302
Grenada	265	281	284	294	310	358	375	357	382
Guyana	64	73	75	107	113	106	92	76	66
Jamaica	1,227	1,497	1,707	1,735	1,693	1,752	1,821	1,904	1,899
St. Kitts and Nevis	110	137	162	172	207	200	170	191	247
St. Lucia	240	312	342	349	390	408	416	559	624
St. Vincent and the Grenadines	133	139	117	126	126	146	121	97	101
Suriname	29	25	16	58	64	64	53	61	55
Trinidad and Tobago	226	251	262	281	311	309	312	356	387
Other Caribbean countries	11,915	12,388	12,913	13,824	14,668	14,856	15,849	17,541	18,126
Cuba	340	424	461	544	617	763	1,004	1,170	1,416
Dominican Republic	1,580	1,467	1,574	1,664	1,817	1,806	2,037	2,482	2,703
Puerto Rico	3,453	3,608	3,773	3,891	4,090	4,055	4,153	4,606	4,705
Others[1]	6,542	6,890	7,106	7,724	8,144	8,232	8,656	9,282	9,302
Memorandum item: Share of independent countries members of CARICOM in total Caribbean (in percent)	40.2	41.2	41.6	40.7	39.7	39.5	38.9	37.6	37.5

Source: Caribbean Tourism Organization.

[1]Includes Anguilla, Aruba, Bermuda, Bonaire, British Virgin Islands, Cayman Islands, Curaçao, Guadeloupe, Haiti, Martinique, Monserrat, Saba, St. Eustasius, St. Maarten, and U.S. Virgin Islands.

Table A5. Caribbean Countries: Stayover Tourist Arrivals
(In thousands)

	1990	1991	1992	1993	1994	1995	1996	1997	1998
Caribbean total	11,731	11,928	12,301	13,359	14,255	14,490	14,905	15,859	16,450
Independent member countries of CARICOM	3,938	3,991	4,086	4,416	4,593	4,698	4,780	4,866	4,862
Antigua and Barbuda	206	205	218	249	263	220	228	240	234
The Bahamas	1,562	1,427	1,399	1,489	1,516	1,598	1,633	1,618	1,540
Barbados	432	394	386	396	426	442	447	472	512
Belize	216	215	247	279	314	321	349	305	288
Dominica	45	46	47	52	57	61	63	65	66
Grenada	82	85	88	94	109	108	108	111	116
Guyana	64	73	75	107	113	106	92	76	66
Jamaica	841	1,007	1,057	1,105	1,098	1,147	1,162	1,192	1,225
St. Kitts and Nevis	76	84	88	89	94	79	84	88	93
St. Lucia	138	159	178	194	219	232	236	248	252
St. Vincent and the Grenadines	54	52	53	57	55	60	58	65	67
Suriname	29	25	16	58	64	64	53	61	55
Trinidad and Tobago	194	220	235	248	266	260	266	324	348
Other Caribbean countries	7,793	7,937	8,215	8,943	9,661	9,792	10,125	10,993	11,588
Cuba	340	424	461	544	617	763	1,004	1,170	1,416
Dominican Republic	1,530	1,417	1,524	1,636	1,767	1,776	1,926	2,211	2,309
Puerto Rico	2,560	2,613	2,754	2,923	3,113	3,054	3,128	3,379	3,461
Others[1]	3,363	3,483	3,477	3,839	4,164	4,200	4,067	4,233	4,402
Memorandum item: Share of independent countries members of CARICOM in total Caribbean (in percent)	33.6	33.5	33.2	33.1	32.2	32.4	32.1	30.7	29.6

Source: Caribbean Tourism Organization.

[1]Includes Anguilla, Aruba, Bermuda, Bonaire, British Virgin Islands, Cayman Islands, Curaçao, Guadeloupe, Haiti, Martinique, Monserrat, Saba, St. Eustasius, St. Maarten, and U.S. Virgin Islands.

Table A6. Caribbean Countries: Cruise Passenger Arrivals[1]
(In thousands)

	1990	1991	1992	1993	1994	1995	1996	1997	1998
Caribbean total	7,394	8,176	8,753	8,858	8,842	8,749	9,687	10,770	10,899
Independent member countries of CARICOM	3,271	3,725	4,055	3,977	3,835	3,685	3,962	4,222	4,362
Antigua and Barbuda	227	256	250	238	236	227	271	286	336
The Bahamas	1,854	2,020	2,139	2,047	1,806	1,544	1,687	1,751	1,730
Barbados	363	372	400	429	460	485	510	518	507
Belize	5	0	2	6	13	8	0	3	14
Dominica	7	65	90	88	126	135	194	230	236
Grenada	183	196	196	200	201	250	267	247	266
Jamaica	386	491	650	630	595	605	658	712	674
St. Kitts and Nevis	34	53	74	83	113	121	86	103	154
St. Lucia	102	153	165	154	172	176	181	310	372
St. Vincent and the Grenadines	79	88	63	69	71	85	63	31	34
Trinidad and Tobago	32	32	27	33	45	49	46	32	39
Other Caribbean countries	4,123	4,452	4,698	4,881	5,006	5,064	5,725	6,548	6,538
Dominican Republic	50	50	50	28	50	31	111	271	394
Puerto Rico	893	995	1,019	968	977	1,001	1,025	1,227	1,243
Others[2]	3,180	3,407	3,629	3,885	3,979	4,032	4,589	5,050	4,901
Memorandum item: Share of independent countries members of CARICOM in total Caribbean (in percent)	44.2	45.6	46.3	44.9	43.4	42.1	40.9	39.2	40.0

Source: Caribbean Tourism Organization.

[1]No information available for cruise ship visitors for Guyana, Suriname, and Cuba.

[2]Includes Anguilla, Aruba, Bermuda, Bonaire, British Virgin Islands, Cayman Islands, Curaçao, Guadeloupe, Haiti, Martinique, Monserrat, Saba, St. Eustasius, St. Maarten, and U.S. Virgin Islands.

Table A7. Caribbean Countries: Number of Hotel Rooms

	1990	1991	1992	1993	1994	1995	1996	1997	1998
Caribbean total	83,774	140,785	150,346	161,210	166,740	174,969	184,315	194,137	205,342
Independent member countries of CARICOM	36,855	51,266	54,416	56,729	58,167	60,149	63,005	63,622	65,498
Antigua and Barbuda	1,350	2,752	3,317	3,317	3,317	3,317	3,185	3,185	3,185
The Bahamas	11,429	13,165	13,541	13,521	13,398	13,421	13,288	13,288	14,243
Barbados	6,680	5,387	5,902	5,580	5,685	5,084	6,315	5,349	5,752
Belize	1,016	2,784	2,913	3,325	3,504	3,708	3,690	3,905	3,921
Dominica	157	547	603	757	757	588	764	824	824
Grenada	570	1,118	1,114	1,428	1,428	1,652	1,669	1,775	1,802
Guyana	538	538	538	538	639	639	639	730	730
Jamaica	10,092	17,337	18,489	18,935	19,760	20,896	21,984	22,954	22,713
St. Kitts and Nevis	584	1,392	1,330	1,600	1,593	1,563	1,610	1,729	1,762
St. Lucia	1,245	2,464	2,659	2,919	2,954	3,974	3,986	3,701	3,769
St. Vincent and the Grenadines	500	1,109	1,164	1,230	1,215	1,176	1,251	1,254	1,550
Suriname	553	532	532	927	967	1,024	1,088	1,276	1,276
Trinidad and Tobago	2,141	2,141	2,314	2,652	2,950	3,107	3,536	3,652	3,971
Other Caribbean countries	46,919	89,519	95,930	104,481	108,573	114,820	121,310	130,515	139,844
Cuba	7,526	16,638	18,682	22,561	23,254	24,233	26,878	31,837	35,708
Dominican Republic	3,800	22,555	24,410	26,801	28,967	32,475	35,729	38,250	42,412
Puerto Rico	9,224	7,897	8,415	8,581	9,519	10,251	10,245	10,849	11,828
Others[1]	26,369	42,429	44,423	46,538	46,833	47,861	48,458	49,579	49,896
Memorandum item: Share of independent countries members of CARICOM in total Caribbean (in percent)	44.0	36.4	36.2	35.2	34.9	34.4	34.2	32.8	31.9

Source: Caribbean Tourism Organization.

[1]Includes Anguilla, Aruba, Bermuda, Bonaire, British Virgin Islands, Cayman Islands, Curaçao, Guadeloupe, Haiti, Martinique, Monserrat, Saba, St. Eustasius, St. Maarten, and U.S. Virgin Islands.

Table A8. Caribbean Countries: Principal Exports[1]
(In percent of total exports)

	1994	1995	1996	1997	1998
The Bahamas					
Food and live animals	31.6	29.1	28.4	26.9	21.1
Nonedible raw materials excluding fuel	16.6	13.8	12.9	13.9	6.2
Chemical products	11.1	7.4	6.9	13.9	11.7
Capital goods	11.4	20.3	13.4	12.4	21.6
Barbados					
Sugar, molasses, and rum	25.4	22.8	19.5	23.6	22.2
Electronic components	19.4	16.6	12.7	12.3	12.9
Chemicals	15.2	15.8	12.8	13.4	13.5
Belize					
Sugar, molasses, and rum	29.1	30.7	30.7	27.5	...
Citrus	10.7	17.7	17.3	13.4	...
Bananas	14.7	13.4	16.8	14.6	...
Dominica					
Bananas	43.9	33.5	32.5	30.1	24.1
Soap	25.9	29.5	33.0	32.1	29.6
Grenada					
Spices	21.0	17.7	24.5	30.8	...
Seafood	12.6	15.6	15.1	14.2	...
Cocoa	12.0	14.3	12.3	7.2	...
Guyana					
Sugar, molasses, and rum	26.0	25.3	26.2	22.5	23.6
Gold	28.6	19.1	18.1	23.1	22.7
Bauxite and alumina	17.6	16.7	15.0	15.1	14.2
Rice	12.4	15.4	16.5	14.2	13.4
Jamaica					
Bauxite and alumina	49.3	40.1	39.5	42.8	43.2
Garments	20.8	15.5	14.3	13.1	12.0
St. Kitts and Nevis					
Machinery and transport equipment	53.4	47.1	50.4	...	...
Sugar, molasses, and rum	33.8	39.3	36.0	...	...
St. Lucia					
Bananas	41.0	40.9	47.0	39.1	37.2
Garments	14.3	12.2	6.9	7.3	7.4
St. Vincent and the Grenadines					
Bananas	30.9	35.3	37.5	31.1	41.5
Flour	17.4	14.0	12.0	18.4	13.9
Rice	12.3	10.3	10.3	12.5	12.9
Suriname					
Bauxite and alumina	72.4	77.0	76.4	77.1	80.5
Seafood	9.9	7.1	7.2	8.4	7.0
Rice	9.1	7.8	7.7	6.4	4.7
Trinidad and Tobago					
Oil and fuels	39.1	45.7	50.3	46.0	48.5
Chemicals	26.6	25.1	22.7	24.0	23.8
Steel products	8.0	8.2	7.1	7.3	8.4

Source: IMF, Recent Economic Developments reports.
[1]Data not available for Antigua and Barbuda.

Table A9. Caribbean Countries: Indicators of Export Performance
(Annual percent change, unless otherwise specified)

	1992	1993	1994	1995	1996	1997	1998
Antigua and Barbuda							
Export volume	12.4	60.8	−12.9	−26.7	33.4	−2.0	16.3
Terms of trade	17.5	−30.5	−15.2	37.3	−66.4	12.7	−5.9
Real effective exchange rate[1]	4.4	4.4	−2.5	−1.4	0.4	5.2	−0.5
Exports of goods/GDP	15.2	13.6	8.9	10.8	7.0	6.5	5.9
Exports of goods and nonfactor services/GDP	96.6	98.9	94.2	86.4	76.3	78.3	73.6
The Bahamas							
Export volume	−6.0	−12.6	1.8	11.9	19.6	6.4	7.6
Terms of trade	−1.5	7.7	0.0	−5.0	0.1	6.1	−0.5
Real effective exchange rate[1]	4.9	1.0	−6.4	−1.2	0.0	3.7	−0.9
Exports of goods/GDP	7.0	5.8	5.1	6.5	6.6	6.2	8.7
Exports of goods and nonfactor services/GDP	50.5	49.7	49.8	50.5	49.5	47.9	49.6
Barbados							
Export volume	2.0	−1.9	7.0	−7.3	8.6	3.7	2.0
Terms of trade	3.8	2.8	−8.4	13.7	2.8	1.1	1.4
Real effective exchange rate[1]	4.3	0.6	−3.7	−1.0	−0.6	5.2	−1.0
Exports of goods/GDP	12.0	11.4	10.9	13.1	14.4	13.1	11.1
Exports of goods and nonfactor services/GDP	55.5	53.7	57.7	62.0	62.5	59.1	56.0
Belize							
Export volume	9.5	−8.1	6.1	2.2	1.9	2.7	2.4
Terms of trade	1.9	11.5	2.1	−4.1	2.0	0.4	0.7
Real effective exchange rate[1]	2.0	5.6	−6.8	0.9	4.2	3.1	−4.3
Exports of goods/GDP	30.7	26.9	28.4	27.8	27.2	30.8	28.4
Exports of goods and nonfactor services/GDP	58.7	54.2	52.0	49.8	49.0	52.6	49.4
Dominica							
Export volume	2.3	−3.9	−4.4	−2.9	5.3	7.5	18.7
Terms of trade	−2.8	−4.6	0.1	−1.4	0.1	2.5	2.6
Real effective exchange rate[1]	4.6	2.0	−3.2	−5.8	1.4	4.8	1.3
Exports of goods/GDP	28.7	24.6	22.2	22.5	22.2	22.0	23.9
Exports of goods and nonfactor services/GDP	51.8	49.0	49.1	49.8	52.2	57.2	56.4
Grenada							
Real effective exchange rate[1]	4.9	5.5	−4.0	−2.2	1.8	3.4	−2.0
Exports of goods/GDP	8.8	8.6	9.4	8.4	7.1	8.2	8.4
Exports of goods and nonfactor services/GDP	31.8	33.9	50.1	49.4	50.7	50.8	47.9
Guyana							
Export volume	30.5	13.4	12.3	−1.7	14.2	13.8	−3.3
Terms of trade	−13.6	2.0	−12.4	2.5	−6.8	−9.7	−0.8
Real effective exchange rate[1]	11.0	4.0	−1.3	5.8	2.4	8.8	−12.5
Exports of goods/GDP	95.0	91.8	82.6	79.9	81.9	79.1	75.8
Exports of goods and nonfactor services/GDP	128.3	118.0	105.0	101.4	101.7	98.8	95.9
Jamaica[2]							
Export volume	1.6	8.8	5.9	32.2	−3.4	−1.5	−4.2
Terms of trade	−7.0	−2.3	6.6	3.5	−7.6	3.4	−2.4
Real effective exchange rate[1]	29.8	−7.9	13.4	1.2	29.2	8.7	2.0
Relative price of tradables to nontradables[3]	−2.6	−27.0	8.0	3.3	−17.0	−8.5	−10.4
Exports of goods/GDP	27.6	31.0	27.7	37.2	26.4	25.3	22.4
Exports of goods and nonfactor services/GDP	61.1	69.6	60.9	70.9	52.7	50.4	48.5
St. Kitts and Nevis							
Export volume	9.7	4.9	−13.2	−3.2	10.4	32.7	−2.3
Terms of trade	4.3	−3.3	0.5	0.1	−1.1	−0.1	1.1
Real effective exchange rate[1]	1.7	1.5	−3.0	0.3	0.7	12.4	−1.8
Relative price of tradables to nontradables[3]	...	−2.4	−2.7	1.8	−2.9	−7.8	...
Exports of goods/GDP	21.5	19.1	20.4	16.8	17.9	22.0	19.3
Exports of goods and nonfactor services/GDP	79.7	75.6	75.7	54.2	58.1	66.0	63.8

Table A9 *(concluded)*

	1992	1993	1994	1995	1996	1997	1998
St. Lucia							
Export volume	20.0	6.2	4.1	5.6	0.7	0.0	7.8
Terms of trade (exclud. tourism)	–4.3	–3.1	–7.0	–5.1	–5.5	7.6	2.9
Real effective exchange rate[1]	4.3	2.1	–0.5	–0.1	–3.4	6.3	–4.4
Exports of goods/GDP	27.0	24.3	19.3	20.3	17.4	14.0	12.9
Exports of goods and nonfactor services/GDP	68.7	68.6	66.6	68.6	65.3	64.1	65.7
St. Vincent and the Grenadines							
Export volume	20.5	–17.8	–7.3	21.3	–10.7	15.4	–8.8
Terms of trade	–8.9	–7.0	2.9	–7.7	3.1	–0.3	–2.0
Real effective exchange rate[1]	3.8	6.4	–5.9	–1.9	3.0	6.7	–1.4
Exports of goods/GDP	31.6	23.3	20.2	23.5	18.9	16.1	15.7
Exports of goods and nonfactor services/GDP	51.4	44.1	46.6	51.6	52.2	48.5	50.4
Suriname							
Export volume	11.1	–19.4	–9.6	28.4	–6.5	22.5	–2.4
Terms of trade	–4.6	0.5	–3.9	–3.1	3.5	–0.8	–0.6
Real effective exchange rate[1]	–30.4	–4.3	6.5	43.5	0.4	22.6	20.4
Exports of goods/GDP	145.0	181.8	91.7	78.6	59.4	65.4	41.1
Exports of goods and nonfactor services/GDP	167.2	218.2	118.0	101.5	69.9	74.3	45.7
Trinidad and Tobago							
Export volume[4]	4.4	–4.3	9.0	22.5	–12.2	2.7	12.1
Terms of trade[4]	–6.9	–6.1	9.5	7.3	1.9	6.3	–13.5
Real effective exchange rate[1]	7.8	–17.0	–2.9	–1.7	–1.7	4.2	3.4
Relative price of tradables to nontradables[3]	...	12.8	21.2	–4.3	1.9	–8.2	–17.8
Exports of goods/GDP[4]	30.5	32.3	39.9	46.5	43.7	43.5	37.2
Exports of goods and nonfactor services/GDP	38.9	40.1	46.5	54.3	51.7	52.8	48.3

Sources: IMF, Recent Economic Developments reports; and IMF staff estimates.

[1]Increase denotes appreciation. Data are end of period.

[2]Data are on fiscal-year basis.

[3]Increase denotes a depreciation.

[4]Excludes re-exports.

Table A10. Caribbean Countries: Imports by Economic Use[1]

(In percent of total imports)

	1994	1995	1996	1997	1998
The Bahamas					
Consumer goods	54.3	51.7	49.1	47.8	45.2
Fuels	13.1	13.6	15.3	12.4	9.8
Raw materials	10.3	10.2	11.1	12.1	15.7
Capital goods	22.3	24.5	24.5	27.7	29.3
Barbados					
Consumer goods	44.2	43.5	41.7	41.6	42.9
Fuels	5.0	4.5	6.1	4.2	5.0
Raw materials	33.6	35.1	31.4	32.2	30.2
Capital goods	16.6	16.3	20.3	22.1	21.8
Belize					
Consumer goods	56.1	51.7	52.0	51.3	56.1
Fuels	8.9	9.3	8.7	8.3	5.6
Raw materials	12.9	12.9	13.8	13.4	12.6
Capital goods	22.1	26.1	25.5	27.0	25.7
Dominica					
Consumer goods	63.2	65.1	60.2	60.4	...
Fuels	6.6	6.0	6.5	6.8	...
Raw materials	9.5	9.6	11.6	9.9	...
Capital goods	20.8	19.3	21.7	22.8	...
Grenada					
Consumer goods	57.6	58.5	56.3	55.4	...
Fuels	7.7	7.8	9.9	7.9	...
Raw materials	12.8	11.9	11.6	10.9	...
Capital goods	21.9	21.8	22.2	25.8	...
Guyana					
Consumer goods	16.3	21.3	28.4	28.3	32.2
Fuels	26.8	16.7	15.1	15.6	12.0
Raw materials	24.6	26.8	27.1	27.2	28.7
Capital goods	21.8	35.0	29.3	28.8	27.0
Jamaica					
Consumer goods	22.0	25.2	25.3	29.7	31.3
Fuels	15.2	13.9	15.7	11.8	9.7
Raw materials	45.3	43.8	39.4	38.6	40.3
Capital goods	17.5	17.2	19.6	19.9	18.7
St. Kitts and Nevis					
Consumer goods	53.3	56.1	55.2	...	...
Fuels	3.1	4.3	5.4	...	...
Raw materials	11.7	11.9	11.5	...	...
Capital goods	32.0	27.7	27.9	...	...
St. Lucia					
Consumer goods	58.8	60.4	56.9	55.4	57.9
Fuels	6.5	7.6	8.2	8.4	8.5
Raw materials	13.0	12.9	13.2	12.2	12.5
Capital goods	21.7	19.1	21.7	24	21.1
St. Vincent and the Grenadines					
Consumer goods	57.8	59.6	57.9	58.5	58.4
Fuels	6.2	6.0	7.2	6.2	5.6
Raw materials	14.6	15.8	15.6	13.4	13.8
Capital goods	21.3	18.5	19.3	21.9	22.2
Suriname					
Consumer goods	23.5	...	...	...	...
Fuels	20.4	...	...	...	...
Raw materials	31.5	...	...	...	...
Capital goods	24.6	...	...	...	...

Table A10 *(concluded)*

	1994	1995	1996	1997	1998
Trinidad and Tobago					
Consumer goods	34.3	21.1	21.1	14.6	17.2
Fuels	19.2	14.4	15.4	10.7	12.7
Raw materials	17.0	26.9	35.3	28.3	30.8
Capital goods	29.5	37.6	28.2	46.3	39.3

Source: IMF, Recent Economic Developments reports.
[1]Data not available for Antigua and Barbuda.

Table A11. Caribbean Countries: Trade Balances
(In percent of GDP)

	1994	1995	1996	1997	1998	Average
Antigua and Barbuda	−52.6	−55.9	−55.7	−50.7	−52.1	−53.4
The Bahamas	−20.9	−26.7	−27.2	−33.0	−32.8	−28.1
Barbados	−20.4	−23.7	−22.9	−30.1	−32.0	−25.8
Belize	−19.1	−17.0	−13.7	−17.4	−19.5	−17.3
Dominica	−22.2	−23.6	−20.2	−20.8	−17.3	−20.8
Grenada	−38.2	−37.0	−42.6	−44.5	−46.3	−41.7
Guyana	−10.9	−6.6	−2.8	−6.6	−7.5	−6.9
Jamaica	−22.6	−18.6	−16.0	−17.0	−16.0	−18.0
St. Kitts and Nevis	−38.2	−37.0	−42.6	−35.6	−46.3	−39.9
St. Lucia	−32.0	−27.7	−31.2	−36.0	−33.0	−32.0
St. Vincent and the Grenadines	−27.5	−21.8	−26.7	−35.5	−37.8	−29.8
Suriname	−2.6	6.8	1.1	3.7	−6.5	0.5
Trinidad and Tobago	12.1	11.1	6.0	−8.4	−12.2	1.7

Source: IMF, Recent Economic Developments reports.

Table A12. Caribbean Countries: Exports and Imports of Goods and Nonfactor Services
(1994–98 averages, in percent of GDP)

	Exports of Goods and Nonfactor Services			Imports of Goods and Nonfactor Services		
	Goods	Nonfactor services	Total	Goods	Nonfactor services	Total
Antigua and Barbuda	7.8	74.0	81.8	61.2	28.1	89.3
The Bahamas	6.6	42.8	49.4	34.7	18.0	52.7
Barbados	13.2	49.7	62.9	39.0	19.8	58.8
Belize	28.5	22.0	50.6	45.9	9.3	55.2
Dominica	22.6	30.4	53.0	43.4	19.2	62.6
Grenada	8.3	41.4	49.7	50.0	11.5	61.5
Guyana	79.9	20.7	100.6	86.8	24.0	110.7
Jamaica	27.8	28.9	56.7	45.8	19.9	65.8
St. Kitts and Nevis	19.3	43.8	63.1	59.2	25.1	84.3
St. Lucia	16.8	49.6	66.3	48.8	22.0	70.8
St. Vincent and the Grenadines	18.9	31.0	49.9	48.7	19.6	68.3
Suriname	67.2	14.6	81.9	66.7	26.1	92.9
Trinidad and Tobago	42.1	8.6	50.7	40.4	4.6	45.0

Sources: IMF, Recent Economic Developments reports; and World Economic Outlook database for The Bahamas.

Table A13. Caribbean Countries: Current Account Balances
(In percent of GDP)

	1994	1995	1996	1997	1998
Antigua and Barbuda	−3.5	−4.6	−18.9	−14.7	−14.4
The Bahamas	−1.1	−4.1	−7.2	−16.7	−22.5
Barbados	7.7	4.8	5.2	0.0	−0.4
Belize	−4.1	−1.7	−1.1	−3.5	−6.2
Dominica	−15.5	−17.0	−12.8	−9.3	−7.0
Grenada	−7.3	−2.1	−8.5	−13.2	−16.5
Guyana	−18.9	−17.9	−9.3	−14.2	−13.1
Jamaica	0.3	−2.5	−1.5	−5.7	−2.9
St. Kitts and Nevis	−11.0	−20.7	−29.9	−24.4	−23.8
St. Lucia	−9.2	−5.4	−10.4	−12.5	−6.7
St. Vincent and the Grenadines	−22.3	−13.8	−9.4	−16.8	−14.0
Suriname	16.2	22.2	1.3	3.0	−10.9
Trinidad and Tobago	4.5	5.1	1.2	−9.9	−10.6

Source: IMF, Recent Economic Developments reports.

Table A14. Caribbean Countries: Gross Domestic Investment[1]
(In percent of GDP)

	1994	1995	1996	1997	1998
Antigua and Barbuda	24.2	33.0	35.0	32.6	32.4
Barbados	14.5	15.1	14.3	16.7	19.2
Belize	24.4	20.0	19.3	23.7	22.8
Dominica	26.9	32.4	29.7	30.0	30.0
Grenada	36.2	31.9	36.1	38.0	40.2
Guyana	27.2	31.8	30.1	30.3	28.7
Jamaica	30.8	31.8	32.3	32.4	29.0
St. Kitts and Nevis	45.2	45.2	45.1	44.9	45.4
St. Lucia	23.9	18.7	21.4	24.6	19.3
St. Vincent and the Grenadines	28.2	30.2	28.3	29.8	31.8
Suriname	15.3	13.4	18.1	21.3	17.8
Trinidad and Tobago	20.2	15.9	16.4	27.1	25.9

Source: IMF, Recent Economic Developments reports.
[1]Data not available for The Bahamas.

Table A15. Consolidated International Claims of BIS Reporting Banks on Caribbean Countries, June 1999

	In Millions of U.S. Dollars	In Percent of GDP
Belize	653	93.9
Dominica	76	27.8
Grenada	36	10.2
Guyana	69	10.1
Jamaica	870	11.9
St. Lucia	87	16.1
St. Vincent and the Grenadines	540	161.0
Suriname	124	15.5
Trinidad and Tobago	1,730	26.5
The Bahamas[1]	16,586	363.1
Barbados[1]	1,980	79.7
Memorandum items:		
Argentina	66,683	23.6
Brazil	62,310	11.2
Mexico	63,776	13.4
Venezuela	13,206	12.9

Source: Bank for International Settlements.

[1]Banking centers according to BIS classification. Belize and most OECS member countries have also developed offshore financial activities.

Table A16. Consolidated International Claims of BIS Reporting Banks on Caribbean Countries by Sector, June 1999

(In percent of total claims)

	Banks	Public Sector	Nonbank Private Sector	Unallocated
Belize	1.4	1.5	97.1	—
Dominica	3.9	6.6	89.5	—
Grenada	22.2	8.3	66.7	2.8
Guyana	13.0	14.5	72.5	—
Jamaica	21.3	33.6	45.2	—
St. Lucia	2.3	1.1	96.6	—
St. Vincent and the Grenadines	0.4	1.3	98.1	0.2
Suriname	15.3	65.3	15.3	4.0
Trinidad and Tobago	5.9	5.8	88.3	—
The Bahamas[1]	40.5	1.9	57.1	0.5
Barbados[1]	18.9	7.6	73.4	—
Memorandum items:				
Developing countries	27.1	18.2	54.4	0.3
Latin America	19.4	22.0	58.4	0.3

Source: Bank for International Settlements.

[1]Banking centers according to BIS classification.

Table A17. Caribbean Countries: Grant Receipts[1]

	1994	1995	1996	1997	1998
	(In percent of GDP)				
Antigua and Barbuda	0.4	0.4	0.7	0.7	1.5
The Bahamas	0.1	0.1	0.0	0.0	0.0
Barbados	0.1	0.1	0.1	0.1	0.2
Belize	1.2	0.1	0.3	1.3	1.2
Dominica	5.3	6.5	8.7	2.1	3.0
Grenada	3.1	2.6	3.8	2.7	4.7
Guyana	4.6	1.9	4.4	5.7	1.6
Jamaica	0.9	0.6	0.5	0.3	0.3
St. Kitts and Nevis[2]	1.1	1.2	0.8	1.2	1.4
St. Lucia	1.3	1.8	1.3	0.5	1.0
St. Vincent and the Grenadines	1.0	0.4	1.0	1.6	4.8
Suriname	22.5	11.9	15.3	8.5	3.8
Trinidad and Tobago[2]	0.2	0.2	0.0	2.3	0.1
	(In percent of central government total revenues and grants)				
Antigua and Barbuda	1.8	1.7	3.2	3.5	6.7
The Bahamas	0.5	0.5	0.1	0.1	0.1
Barbados	0.3	0.3	0.3	0.3	0.6
Belize	4.8	0.4	1.3	5.4	4.8
Dominica	16.9	19.4	22.8	6.7	9.3
Grenada	11.4	9.3	13.2	10.1	15.4
Guyana	12.6	5.4	11.2	15.2	5.0
Jamaica	3.1	2.0	1.8	1.1	1.0
St. Kitts and Nevis[2]	4.0	3.9	2.6	3.8	4.6
St. Lucia	4.9	7.2	5.1	1.9	3.6
St. Vincent and the Grenadines	3.4	1.5	3.4	5.3	14.4
Suriname	44.1	29.2	35.3	25.3	11.8
Trinidad and Tobago[2]	0.8	0.7	0.1	8.3	0.3

Source: IMF, Recent Economic Developments reports.

[1]For some countries, the fiscal year begins on April 1 or July 1 (see Table 8).

[2]Capital revenue and grants.

Table A18. Caribbean Countries: Banking Intermediation
(In percent of GDP)

	1992	1993	1994	1995	1996	1997	1998
				(Bank deposits)[1]			
Antigua and Barbuda	57.5	58.6	59.5	73.2	64.3	64.9	...
The Bahamas	44.6	52.6	53.5	58.1	...	...	...
Barbados	50.8	50.6	52.5	51.2	57.2	57.1	57.7
Belize	37.1	34.9	36.5	41.2	43.1	48.0	52.7
Dominica	57.2	54.0	53.3	63.4	64.2	65.1	...
Grenada	52.3	65.5	69.8	84.6	75.4	77.9	81.9
Guyana	54.3	51.0	44.7	48.7	52.8	53.9	...
Jamaica	41.7	41.5	44.1	45.2	41.9	43.5	41.1
St. Kitts and Nevis	70.2	70.9	64.1	71.2	68.1	72.0	...
St. Lucia	51.8	52.7	56.4	58.1	59.2	61.3	...
St. Vincent and the Grenadines	49.7	53.2	54.9	54.0	55.1	59.4	...
Suriname	36.2	29.5	15.0	16.1	10.9	13.3	12.2
Trinidad and Tobago	36.3	39.9	39.1	37.6	42.4	44.6	...
				(Bank lending)[2]			
Antigua and Barbuda	51.3	48.5	45.5	53.0	58.0	65.2	...
The Bahamas	42.5	49.1	52.1	57.9	...	...	...
Barbados	35.2	34.2	36.5	39.4	38.5	42.1	45.7
Belize	38.4	36.4	36.7	37.3	39.6	44.2	51.9
Dominica	51.0	53.5	53.7	57.3	56.2	59.0	...
Grenada	46.5	61.3	58.5	67.7	62.3	69.2	75.6
Guyana	18.7	17.3	18.4	23.9	36.7	42.4	...
Jamaica	19.6	23.4	24.3	26.1	25.6	26.1	29.8
St. Kitts and Nevis	68.2	70.2	69.5	70.8	70.2	72.0	...
St. Lucia	51.0	56.1	61.7	63.9	70.0	76.0	...
St. Vincent and the Grenadines	41.3	41.4	43.7	48.9	53.8	58.2	...
Suriname	49.1	28.2	10.2	10.5	19.7	23.8	26.5
Trinidad and Tobago	33.4	32.6	26.0	27.7	28.0	32.3	...
				(Stock market capitalization)			
Barbados	16.4	20.0	30.0	26.6	38.8	52.5	103.7
Jamaica	88.4	29.1	27.2	26.2	29.4	33.5	30.3
Trinidad and Tobago	9.4	11.5	13.4	21.3	25.5	54.3	67.3

Sources: IMF, *International Financial Statistics;* and IMF staff estimates.
[1]Demand, and time and savings deposits, in local and foreign currency.
[2]Claims on private sector of deposit money banks.

Table A19. Caribbean Countries: Central Government Balances[1]

(Overall balances after grants, in percent of GDP)

	1994	1995	1996	1997	1998
Antigua and Barbuda	−5.4	−4.9	−1.7	−4.5	−3.9
The Bahamas	−1.0	−0.9	−1.7	−3.4	−2.0
Barbados	−0.3	−0.3	−3.9	−0.8	−0.7
Belize	−6.0	−3.4	−2.5	−2.4	−3.8
Dominica	−5.7	−0.4	−0.8	−4.6	−3.8
Grenada	−3.5	−0.6	−3.7	−6.2	−3.5
Guyana	0.9	−3.9	−0.6	−5.0	−6.8
Jamaica	2.8	1.5	−6.5	−8.3	−7.5
St. Kitts and Nevis	−2.0	−2.4	−3.9	−4.6	−7.7
St. Lucia	−0.7	−1.0	−1.4	−1.9	−1.1
St. Vincent and the Grenadines	−1.0	0.5	0.2	−4.5	−2.1
Suriname	−2.5	1.1	2.3	−5.2	−11.1
Trinidad and Tobago	0.0	0.2	−0.5	0.1	−1.8

Source: IMF, Recent Economic Developments reports.

[1]For some countries, the fiscal year begins on April 1 or July 1 (see Table 8).

Table A20. Caribbean Countries: Central Government—Total Revenue and Grants[1]
(In percent of GDP)

	1994	1995	1996	1997	1998
Antigua and Barbuda	21.0	21.3	22.5	21.4	21.7
Revenue	20.6	20.9	21.8	20.6	20.3
Of which:					
Tax revenue	17.5	17.8	18.5	17.9	17.6
Grants	0.4	0.4	0.7	0.7	1.5
The Bahamas	18.8	19.1	18.4	18.5	18.4
Revenue	18.7	19.0	18.3	18.5	18.4
Of which:					
Tax revenue	16.5	16.7	16.5	16.7	16.5
Grants	0.1	0.1	0.0	0.0	0.0
Barbados	29.2	29.7	29.8	32.1	32.2
Revenue	29.1	29.6	29.7	32.0	32.0
Of which:					
Tax revenue	27.0	27.8	27.7	30.7	30.0
Grants	0.1	0.1	0.1	0.1	0.2
Belize	25.0	22.5	24.3	24.1	24.6
Revenue	23.8	22.4	24.0	22.8	23.5
Of which:					
Tax revenue	20.6	19.4	19.8	19.6	19.7
Grants	1.2	0.1	0.3	1.3	1.2
Dominica	31.3	33.5	38.1	31.2	32.3
Revenue	26.0	27.0	29.4	29.1	29.3
Of which:					
Tax revenue	22.0	23.3	23.5	23.4	23.8
Grants	5.3	6.5	8.7	2.1	3.0
Grenada	27.2	28.3	28.8	26.8	30.3
Revenue	24.1	25.7	25.0	24.1	25.4
Of which:					
Tax revenue	21.8	22.6	22.7	21.9	22.7
Grants	3.1	2.6	3.8	2.7	4.7
Guyana	36.6	35.2	39.2	37.6	32.1
Revenue	32.0	33.3	34.8	31.9	30.5
Of which:					
Tax revenue	29.8	31.4	32.3	29.6	28.6
Grants	4.6	1.9	4.4	5.7	1.6
Jamaica	29.2	30.4	28.3	27.5	29.1
Revenue	28.3	29.8	27.8	27.2	28.8
Of which:					
Tax revenue	24.9	26.1	24.8	24.5	26.3
Grants	0.9	0.6	0.5	0.3	0.3
St. Kitts and Nevis	27.7	31.0	31.0	31.6	30.6
Revenue	26.6	29.8	30.2	30.4	29.2
Of which:					
Tax revenue	21.1	21.3	21.6	22.4	21.8
Grants	1.1	1.2	0.8	1.2	1.4
St. Lucia	25.9	25.8	25.6	24.7	27.4
Revenue	24.7	24.0	24.3	24.2	26.4
Of which:					
Tax revenue	22.2	21.8	21.4	21.6	23.7
Grants	1.3	1.8	1.3	0.5	1.0

Table A20 *(concluded)*

	1994	1995	1996	1997	1998
St. Vincent and the Grenadines	29.2	27.3	29.1	30.1	33.4
Revenue	28.2	26.9	28.1	28.5	28.6
Of which:					
Tax revenue	23.9	23.2	24.3	24.3	24.6
Grants	1.0	0.4	1.0	1.6	4.8
Suriname	51.1	40.7	43.3	33.7	32.1
Revenue	28.5	28.8	28.0	25.1	28.3
Of which:					
Tax revenue	22.5	25.1	25.3	21.2	23.0
Grants	22.5	11.9	15.3	8.5	3.8
Trinidad and Tobago	25.8	26.9	27.7	27.2	25.4
Revenue	25.6	26.7	27.7	25.0	25.3
Of which:					
Tax revenue[2]	22.6	24.5	25.4	22.4	22.0
Grants[3]	0.2	0.2	0.0	2.3	0.1

Source: IMF, Recent Economic Developments reports.

[1]For some countries, the fiscal year begins on April 1 or July 1 (see Table 8).

[2]Includes oil and non-oil taxes.

[3]Capital revenue and grants.

Table A21. Caribbean Countries: Central Government Expenditure[1]
(In percent of GDP)

	1994	1995	1996	1997	1998
Antigua and Barbuda[2]	26.4	26.2	24.3	25.9	25.6
Wages and salaries	11.1	11.5	11.1	10.6	11.6
Interest payments	3.4	3.2	3.2	4.3	3.1
The Bahamas	19.7	20.1	20.0	21.9	20.4
Wages and salaries	9.8	9.8	8.9	9.3	9.3
Interest payments	2.3	2.3	2.3	2.4	2.4
Barbados[2]	30.0	30.0	32.7	33.0	32.9
Wages and salaries	11.4	11.3	11.7	11.3	10.9
Interest payments	4.5	4.8	4.8	4.4	4.6
Belize	30.9	25.9	26.8	26.5	29.1
Wages and salaries	11.7	11.0	10.5	9.9	10.2
Interest payments	1.9	1.9	2.0	1.9	2.0
Dominica	37.0	33.9	38.9	35.8	36.1
Wages and salaries	14.8	14.2	15.5	14.7	14.7
Interest payments	2.4	2.4	3.0	2.7	2.5
Grenada	30.7	28.8	32.5	33.0	33.7
Wages and salaries	12.0	12.1	12.2	12.9	11.4
Interest payments	2.4	2.0	2.2	2.3	1.6
Guyana	35.8	39.1	39.8	42.6	38.7
Wages and salaries	6.0	6.3	6.6	7.8	8.4
Interest payments	10.1	10.1	7.6	9.5	8.0
Jamaica	26.4	28.9	34.9	35.8	36.6
Wages and salaries	7.3	8.2	10.8	12.0	12.5
Interest payments	9.8	9.3	12.2	10.2	13.7
St. Kitts and Nevis	29.7	33.4	34.9	36.2	38.3
Wages and salaries	12.6	13.9	14.8	14.1	14.8
Interest payments	2.5	2.2	3.0	2.8	3.1
St. Lucia[2]	26.6	26.8	27.0	26.6	30.7
Wages and salaries	9.9	11.3	10.8	11.0	10.9
Interest payments	0.7	0.8	0.9	1.0	1.3
St. Vincent and the Grenadines[2]	30.2	26.8	28.9	34.5	35.5
Wages and salaries	13.0	12.7	12.8	13.0	12.8
Interest payments	1.3	1.7	1.7	1.6	1.6
Suriname[2]	44.5	39.2	41.0	38.8	41.2
Wages and salaries	8.4	7.2	9.4	13.2	16.1
Interest payments	3.2	0.8	0.9	0.5	0.6
Trinidad and Tobago[2]	25.8	26.7	28.2	27.1	27.2
Wages and salaries	9.4	9.1	10.1	8.8	9.2
Interest payments	5.4	5.0	4.6	4.6	5.0
Average for the region[3]	30.3	29.7	31.5	32.1	32.8
Wages and salaries	10.6	10.7	11.2	11.4	11.8
Interest payments	3.8	3.6	3.7	3.7	3.8

Source: IMF, Recent Economic Developments reports.

[1]For some countries, the fiscal year begins on April 1 or July 1 (see Table 8).

[2]Total expenditure and net lending.

[3]Unweighted average.

Bibliography

Errico, Luca, and Alberto Musalem, 1999, "Offshore Banking: An Amalgam of Micro- and Macro-Prudential Issues," IMF Working Paper No. 99/5 (Washington: International Monetary Fund).

Neary, J. Peter, and Sweder van Wijnbergen, eds., 1986, *Natural Resources and the Macroeconomy* (Cambridge, Massachusetts: MIT Press).

Organization for Economic Cooperation and Development, 1998, *Harmful Tax Competition: An Emerging Global Issue* (Paris).

Randall, Ruby, 1998, "Interest Rate Spreads in the Eastern Caribbean," IMF Working Paper No. 98/59 (Washington: International Monetary Fund).

Woodward, Douglas P., and Robert J. Rolfe, 1993, "The Location of Export-Oriented Foreign Direct Investment in the Caribbean Basin," *Journal of International Business Studies,* Vol. 24, No. 1, pp. 121–44.

van Beek, Frits, José Roberto Rosales, Mayra Zermeño, Ruby Randall, and Jorge Shepherd, 2000, *The Eastern Caribbean Currency Union: Institutions, Performance, and Policy Issues*, IMF Occasional Paper No. 195 (Washington: International Monetary Fund).

World Bank, 1998, *Wider Caribbean Financial Sector Review—Increasing Competitiveness and Financial Resource Management for Economic Growth* (Washington).

———, 2000, "The Management of Catastrophic Risks Using Pooled Insurance Structures and Alternative Financing and Risk Transfer Mechanisms—The Reinsurance Market and the Case of the Caribbean Basin," Working Paper Draft (Washington).

Recent Occasional Papers of the International Monetary Fund

177. Perspectives on Regional Unemployment in Europe, by Paolo Mauro, Eswar Prasad, and Antonio Spilimbergo. 1999.

176. Back to the Future: Postwar Reconstruction and Stabilization in Lebanon, edited by Sena Eken and Thomas Helbling. 1999.

175. Macroeconomic Developments in the Baltics, Russia, and Other Countries of the Former Soviet Union, 1992–97, by Luis M. Valdivieso. 1998.

174. Impact of EMU on Selected Non–European Union Countries, by R. Feldman, K. Nashashibi, R. Nord, P. Allum, D. Desruelle, K. Enders, R. Kahn, and H. Temprano-Arroyo. 1998.

173. The Baltic Countries: From Economic Stabilization to EU Accession, by Julian Berengaut, Augusto Lopez-Claros, Françoise Le Gall, Dennis Jones, Richard Stern, Ann-Margret Westin, Effie Psalida, Pietro Garibaldi. 1998.

172. Capital Account Liberalization: Theoretical and Practical Aspects, by a staff team led by Barry Eichengreen and Michael Mussa, with Giovanni Dell'Ariccia, Enrica Detragiache, Gian Maria Milesi-Ferretti, and Andrew Tweedie. 1998.

171. Monetary Policy in Dollarized Economies, by Tomás Baliño, Adam Bennett, and Eduardo Borensztein. 1998.

170. The West African Economic and Monetary Union: Recent Developments and Policy Issues, by a staff team led by Ernesto Hernández-Catá and comprising Christian A. François, Paul Masson, Pascal Bouvier, Patrick Peroz, Dominique Desruelle, and Athanasios Vamvakidis. 1998.

169. Financial Sector Development in Sub-Saharan African Countries, by Hassanali Mehran, Piero Ugolini, Jean Phillipe Briffaux, George Iden, Tonny Lybek, Stephen Swaray, and Peter Hayward. 1998.

168. Exit Strategies: Policy Options for Countries Seeking Greater Exchange Rate Flexibility, by a staff team led by Barry Eichengreen and Paul Masson with Hugh Bredenkamp, Barry Johnston, Javier Hamann, Esteban Jadresic, and Inci Ötker. 1998.

167. Exchange Rate Assessment: Extensions of the Macroeconomic Balance Approach, edited by Peter Isard and Hamid Faruqee. 1998

166. Hedge Funds and Financial Market Dynamics, by a staff team led by Barry Eichengreen and Donald Mathieson with Bankim Chadha, Anne Jansen, Laura Kodres, and Sunil Sharma. 1998.

165. Algeria: Stabilization and Transition to the Market, by Karim Nashashibi, Patricia Alonso-Gamo, Stefania Bazzoni, Alain Féler, Nicole Laframboise, and Sebastian Paris Horvitz. 1998.

164. MULTIMOD Mark III: The Core Dynamic and Steady-State Model, by Douglas Laxton, Peter Isard, Hamid Faruqee, Eswar Prasad, and Bart Turtelboom. 1998.

163. Egypt: Beyond Stabilization, Toward a Dynamic Market Economy, by a staff team led by Howard Handy. 1998.

162. Fiscal Policy Rules, by George Kopits and Steven Symansky. 1998.

161. The Nordic Banking Crises: Pitfalls in Financial Liberalization? by Burkhard Drees and Ceyla Pazarbaşıoğlu. 1998.

160. Fiscal Reform in Low-Income Countries: Experience Under IMF-Supported Programs, by a staff team led by George T. Abed and comprising Liam Ebrill, Sanjeev Gupta, Benedict Clements, Ronald McMorran, Anthony Pellechio, Jerald Schiff, and Marijn Verhoeven. 1998.

159. Hungary: Economic Policies for Sustainable Growth, Carlo Cottarelli, Thomas Krueger, Reza Moghadam, Perry Perone, Edgardo Ruggiero, and Rachel van Elkan. 1998.

158. Transparency in Government Operations, by George Kopits and Jon Craig. 1998.

157. Central Bank Reforms in the Baltics, Russia, and the Other Countries of the Former Soviet Union, by a staff team led by Malcolm Knight and comprising Susana Almuiña, John Dalton, Inci Otker, Ceyla Pazarbaşıoğlu, Arne B. Petersen, Peter Quirk, Nicholas M. Roberts, Gabriel Sensenbrenner, and Jan Willem van der Vossen. 1997.

Note: For information on the title and availability of Occasional Papers not listed, please consult the IMF Publications Catalog or contact IMF Publication Services.